Suzie Hayman trained as a teach
she joined the Family Plannin_
subsequently becoming press officer. She was information officer for
Brook Advisory Centres from 1976 to 1984 and since then has
become a freelance journalist and broadcaster. She is now a Board
member of Brook Advisory Centres as well as being a member of the
Family Planning Association's National Executive; her FPA endorsed
book *Guide to Contraception* was published in May 1993. Suzie
Hayman has written for many national magazines including *Woman
and Home*, *Good Housekeeping*, *Bella* and *Country Living* as well as
for the *Guardian* and *Sunday Times* newspapers. She is currently
'agony aunt' for *Woman's Own* magazine. Her books include *It's
More than Sex: A Survival Guide to the Teenage Years*, *Hysterec-
tomy*, *Living with a Teenager*, *The Well Woman Handbook*
(Penguin 1989) and *Endometriosis* (Penguin 1991). She is a frequent
contributor to television and radio and lives in Cumbria with her
partner and three cats.

Other People's Children

SUZIE HAYMAN

PENGUIN BOOKS

PENGUIN BOOKS

Published by the Penguin Group
Penguin Books Ltd, 27 Wrights Lane, London w8 5tz, England
Penguin Books USA Inc., 375 Hudson Street, New York, New York 10014, USA
Penguin Books Australia Ltd, Ringwood, Victoria, Australia
Penguin Books Canada Ltd, 10 Alcorn Avenue, Toronto, Ontario, Canada m4v 3b2
Penguin Books (NZ) Ltd, 182–190 Wairau Road, Auckland 10, New Zealand

Penguin Books Ltd, Registered Offices: Harmondsworth, Middlesex, England

First published 1994
1 3 5 7 9 10 8 6 4 2

Set by Datix International Limited, Bungay, Suffolk
Printed in England by Clays Ltd, St Ives plc
Set in 10½/13 pt Monophoto Sabon

To my beloved
Other Person's Child,
and to his father

Contents

Acknowledgements

I would like to thank the many people whose stories I have used to illustrate the position of the new, extended family today. Most of all, I would like to acknowledge and thank Alex Cowan for his suggestions, additional research and interviews. In more ways than one, this book would not have been possible without him.

Introduction

When our politicians talk of 'the family', they invariably mean an idealized unit of two adults, married and living together, bringing up their own children. If your family does not conform to this narrow definition, you can find yourself feeling alone and out of step. However, a brief look around could show you that many households among your neighbours, your friends and your relatives are very different from this idealized image. Yet most of us whose families do not conform still suffer from the feeling that we are in a minority of one. We are often too ashamed to talk about how this affects us.

The effects are wide-ranging and often severe. As an agony aunt, a counsellor and someone in a step-relationship, I know from my personal experience and from the experiences of many of my readers and clients that being part of a stepfamily can be painful and confusing, whatever your role. Being in such a situation is one problem; feeling different or like an outsider is another.

Step-relationships do not have to be quite as destructive as some of us anticipate or find. I make no promises, but I hope that by shedding some light on the number of stepfamilies, by exploring the problems, discussing why they may arise and making some suggestions as to what you can do about them, this book may help anyone experiencing difficulties in this form of relationship. Twenty years ago, I met my partner and began a relationship not only with him but with his son by his previous marriage. I am sure it would have helped all of us if we had been able to read *Other People's Children* at that time. I wrote the book for all the Suzies, Vics and Alexes still out there, knowing that it is never too late to learn from your own or other people's mistakes and to do better.

I

You Are Not Alone

'I married John five years ago and I remember thinking on our wedding day how wonderful it was to have a built-in family waiting for me. Martin was eight and Emma was six at the time, and they came to the wedding all dressed up and looking so sweet. It was only afterwards that I realized that my friends and family studiously avoided making any comment about the fact that these children were now *mine*. About a week or so after the wedding, the problems started. But, you see, the difficulty was that I couldn't talk to anyone about what was going on. I felt as if we were utterly different, utterly unique, and I had no one I knew in the same situation to talk to. I was out on a limb, all alone, and I felt truly desperate.'

'Dad's girlfriend came to live with us when I was eleven, in the summer before I started secondary school. I went into this class and as far as I knew I was the only one who didn't have a real mother. I hated it. I couldn't talk about it or tell anyone how I felt, and I didn't want to make real friends because that would mean I would have to bring them home and I didn't want awkward questions. The worst thing was that I know my dad and Sheila were quite open about it all when they went to parent–teacher meetings, but the teachers still seemed to insist on pretending that she was my real mother. That sort of sent the message to me that saying any different was definitely out. It wasn't until the fifth form, when we had a teacher who did a whole project with us on families, that I found out that half the class were like me, not living in your bog-standard, average family with a natural mum and dad. But it was a bit bloody late then, wasn't it? I'd wasted five years feeling bitter, twisted and alone.'

The very first barrier to overcome when adjusting to being part of a stepfamily is the belief that you are in any way unusual. Stepfamilies are as old as any other family unit and are hardly uncommon. Long before we learned to make written records children lost parents, spouses lost partners and new ones took their place. What is interesting is that our almost universally unfavourable view of stepfamilies interferes not only with our understanding of what happens in them but even with our recognition of their existence. We do not know for certain how many people are members of stepfamilies in our society today, and there are two main reasons for this.

One is that up to now 'the powers that be' have been too embarrassed to ask. The last Census did not find out about the exact relationship between children in a household and the adults presumed to be their parents. The answers to the questions asked showed how many adults and how many children there were in this country, and in which households they mainly lived. The Census thus produced a figure for 'parents and their children', but did not establish whether these units were families by blood, adoption or second marriage. According to the Office of Population Censuses and Surveys:

> The general feeling [in the unit concerned with social statistics] is that there is a reluctance to ask official questions about such a sensitive area of family relationships.

The only relevant comment made in *Britain's Children* (OPCS Census Guide 2 of 1985) is:

> With the higher level of divorce and remarriage in the 1970s, the number of children with one or both parents in a second (or later) marriage must have grown rapidly. In 1981, among married couples in which the wife

4

was in her 30s, for about 1 in 7, one or both of the couple were in a second marriage. Not all these couples would have children from the earlier marriage(s), but this is a reminder that the proportion of all children who have a step-parent . . . is sizeable.

We can make intelligent estimates as to the number of stepfamilies. We know, for instance, that at the moment around 150,000 couples divorce every year. Over half of the marriages ending in divorce have children, and the number of children involved is over 200,000. We also know that 50 per cent of divorcees remarry within five years of the ending of their first marriage – 1 in 3 of the 350,000 marriages in England and Wales each year is a remarriage for one or both partners. So it would appear that in the UK around 6 million people, or almost 10 per cent of the population, are in a step-relationship at present. The General Household Survey (1991) asked a representative sample of both men and women if they had any stepchildren or adopted or foster children living with them, and concluded that 8 per cent of families fell into this category.

But do these estimated figures give a full picture of how numerous stepfamilies are? Divorce statistics will not account for the children whose parents were living together but were not married, or those children whose parents were married but separated without a formal divorce. We count children only when their parents divorce, not when they remarry, and we have no figures for how many children are part of families in which a spouse has died and the surviving partner remarried.

The second reason for the unclear picture hinges on a general lack of agreement over the exact definition of the term 'stepfamily'. The General Household Survey counted children even when the adults caring for them were cohabiting and did not insist that the relationship be called 'step' only if they were married. However, we tend to define a step-family as a unit in which the children live full time; the adults caring for them are the step-parents and the children are the stepchildren. Adding up the people concerned in this way accounts for just one household, and ignores the fact that in a divided family the child often has a link with two households, both of which are 'stepfamily' households. An estranged father's new partner is just as much involved in a step-relationship with his children as is their mother's new partner who lives with them permanently. Their mother too will be in a step-relationship if her estranged husband has children in his new family or if her new partner has children in his old one. You are a step-parent if the children you care for are seen by you once a week, once a month, sometime or never, just as much as if they live with you.

When all the possible variations are considered, it would seem that the number of people in step-relationships in this country is probably nearer to eighteen million, or almost one in three people. We may not be in the majority, but we are members of a very large group, not isolated, lonely and unusual freaks. Very few 'minority' groups can claim to comprise a third of the population.

The figure that represents how many people are affected by step-relationships has to be far greater even than eighteen million, because step-relationships do not stop at the front door. If you live with or are linked in some way to someone else's children, then your parents, your siblings, your aunts and uncles, your friends, your neighbours, your colleagues and your employers are also affected to varying degrees by what this means in your life. Ask around you. I have, and I have yet to find anyone whose life is not in some way touched by such a relationship, whether they or someone they know is caring for or is someone else's child.

Stepfamilies take many forms. New partnerships are made after separation, divorce or the death of a spouse or living companion and may or may not be formalized by marriage. One or both partners may have children, who may live with the new partnership or remain with the ex-partner, being seen only on certain occasions. In all these families, and in families where children are fostered or adopted, adults will find themselves caring for other people's children.

Literature and history are full of references to stepfamilies. The question is not whether they exist, because we all know they do, but how we view them and what place we consider they take in our landscape. These new relationships are becoming more visible and we are trying as a society to acknowledge and understand them. Part of that process is finding ways of describing them. One of our problems is that while 'the family' has very positive values attached to it (sometimes unreasonably), the words 'stepfamily' or 'step-parent' have very negative connotations. You can see that 'stepfamily' and 'step-parent' may be inadequate to encompass the diverse range of relationships between children and adults in present-day society. If the step-relationship is considered, accurately or not, to exist only where the children and adults live together and the adults are married, it simply does not cover everyone involved. And the sad thing, as many people who have found themselves in this position can confirm, is that if we have no word for something, we often do not acknowledge it has any reality.

Gemma is twenty-seven and has been married to George for three years. George has a seven-year-old daughter and a five-year-old son, both living with his ex-wife. Gemma explained her relationship with his 'invisible' first family:

When I married George, I knew that he had two children by his previous marriage. But since he only saw them four or five times a year and I'd only heard about them and never met them in the two years we were going out together, I was totally unprepared for how much they would affect our marriage. These two children and their mother were an ever present drain on our resources, both emotional and financial. But the worst part was that none of my friends, my parents or anyone I knew could see or understand what they did to us. They weren't part of our family. They never stayed with us. They never went anywhere with us where our friends or relatives could see them. They were simply invisible. How could I explain that they were there, that we were related and that they were part of our family just by existing?

Rather than 'stepfamilies', counsellors and workers in the field of personal relationships now talk of 're-formed', 'reconstituted' or 'blended' families. We could also describe the somewhat confused network of formal and informal relationships as 'new extended families'. The extended family takes in all the relationships around the nuclear family of mother, father and their children – that is, grandparents, aunts, uncles, cousins, brothers, sisters, nieces and nephews. A new extended family would include new partners and their relatives as well as old partners and their relatives.

Blended families are neither new nor particularly unusual, since diversity is far more common than we like to admit. Families formed in different ways from the standard 'two parents + two children' stereotype would seem to be growing in number. Just look at the figures. At any one time only one in twenty households is a so-called 'typical' family of a breadwinner father and a stay-at-home mother bringing up their own two children. Most families at some time pass through a stage of fitting into this pattern, but by the year

2000 only 50 per cent of young people will have spent their entire childhood in what many of us still consider a 'normal' home life. And this, of course, is the fundamental problem for the blended family: while the relationship may have inbuilt difficulties, much of the friction and tension arises because it is operating in a world that continues to assume the existence of a traditional family that has long gone.

In reality the 'family' is a much more elastic concept. A family can consist of two adults, married or unmarried, whose children have grown up and left them; of two adults of the same sex who have children; of two adults of the opposite sex who have no children; of a single parent whose partner has left or died, bringing up children on his or her own; or of elderly parents cared for by a single adult child. All these are just as much 'families' as the ideal stereotype. More important to our discussion, a family can also consist of two adults, married or unmarried, caring full time for children who are related by blood to just one, or caring part time for children who stay only at weekends or during school holidays; or, indeed, of two adults with full-time and part-time children of each partner. Families, in other words, are units in which one or both of the adults can be called upon to love and care for other people's children.

Even though as many as one in three people in the UK today are involved in some sort of reconstituted family, often the only pictures of what a step-parent is and what a stepchild can expect are to be found in fairy tales, such as 'Cinderella' and 'Hansel and Gretel', which hardly give an encouraging view. It is not surprising, then, that the situation can be a tricky one. There may be many occasions in your life when you find yourself taking on responsibility once held by another person and stepping into someone else's shoes. You could be given a job which used to be done by someone else or move into a house previously occupied by

9

others. If something is not brand new, the shadow of the person who was there before may always be there. You may find it uncomfortable to see the signs of your predecessor's occupancy and resent it when other people remark on how it used to be. You may start to change things deliberately, not because they need changing but just to make your own mark. None of these situations gives rise to quite the confused feelings, reactions and behaviour that occur when taking on other people's children or having your own children accept into their lives an adult who is not their original parent. You may find that you have all the discomfort and resentment mentioned above, but that the consequences are not the same as when you just changed the wallpaper in your new house.

Most adults who are thrown into a relationship with other people's children feel guilty about any troubles they have; they cannot discuss any anxieties or antagonisms, and feel isolated and alone. Most young people faced with a parent's new partner often have even less support or opportunity for discussion.

So, what are the problems you may encounter? Whatever the circumstances, these relationships often suffer from inherent difficulties, even before you begin to consider the clashes that can arise between differing individuals. The child comes as part of the package, rather than being chosen or planned, and the relationship between the new adult and the child may have no time to develop before being seen as a full-blown 'parent and child' relationship. In first-time families the couple get to know each other and learn to live with each other before children appear. The order of events is reversed in a re-formed family. Neither new parent nor child may have a clear idea of what is expected from them or the relationship. Who is in charge, who is responsible and what do you call each other? Is he or she 'Dad' or 'Mum' or what?

Children may be a painful reminder to their parent of a bitter or unhappy liaison, or an uncomfortable reminder to a step-parent that someone was there before. The child will almost certainly have loyalties and often mixed feelings towards the other birth parent – including anger, loss and guilt – which may not be understood but may be evident in bad behaviour or unhappiness. In addition, the circumstances that create a blended family are often related to tragedy, bitterness, anger or a sense of failure. This makes it all the more difficult for you to talk about your anxieties or seek any help.

Our society places enormous value on blood relationships and sees them as more desirable, more significant and more important than any other kind of tie between adult and child. Forming a happy bond between an adult and a non-related child may be very hard, both because of their own feelings and because of the lack of support and understanding from other people. There is often an enormous loss of self-esteem in all members of a blended family just because they are what they are. Men, whether original fathers or stepfathers, may have a rosier picture of what is happening within their reconstituted family than their partners. The children and the women are often the ones to bear the brunt of any difficulties.

The success of any family depends on the emotional responses of everyone concerned. The drawback in a re-formed family is that so many different viewpoints have to be taken into account. When you marry for the first time, you have to think of yourself and your partner, and then widen your scope to encompass your family, your friends, the community and society at large. The attitudes of all these people will have some effect on whether or not your partnership works. In a re-formed family the new layers are those of your children, any ex-partners and their families.

Hostility may be directed towards one particular person by other members of this new extended family, and how everyone around you approaches re-formed families may affect your chances of success.

Some people find the marriage seems doomed before it has even begun. Thirteen years ago Leonora married Andrew, who is twenty-five years older than her. She brought two children to the relationship and he had four, all of whom were married with children of their own.

His children are grown up and his grandchildren are teenagers. To be honest, I don't know how I've lasted this long and I've no intention of battling any longer. Hardly a week has gone by in that thirteen years when his son or one of his three daughters hasn't been unpleasant to me. They ring me up and are abusive, and they have become more and more unpleasant as the years have passed. They accuse me of stealing his money, of turning him against them, of being in their way, when the facts are just the opposite. I support him – he's been retired for the last seven years. There have been times when he's had rows and feuds with them, and I've been the one to urge him to make up. At first, when everyone was telling me that they'd seen off girlfriends in the past and I didn't have a hope, I said that it was just a case of their missing their mother and they'd come round to me in the end. They never will, I now realize. He'll argue with them, but he won't hear a word against them from me or anyone else and he's about as unsupportive as you can imagine. Now my own children have left for college, I've decided that I owe myself something better out of life. I don't understand why I didn't do it earlier, but I suppose I hoped things would get better.

For others, a re-formed family seems to have been a made-in-heaven bed of roses. Graham and Lis married eighteen months ago after meeting on holiday, and his three children live with them. Lis says:

> It was a whirlwind romance. We saw each other for about six months after we came back before we finally decided to get married. In that time it had never occurred to me to exclude his three children from consideration. Even on some of our evening dates they came too, or we would have dinner at his house if he couldn't get a babysitter. Certainly they'd be there on the weekends. Don't get the idea that we didn't have privacy. We did, it was just that I knew from the beginning that I was getting a unit of four rather than a man on his own.
>
> I suppose we've had some problems, but what family doesn't? I've had to fit in with some of their routines and introduce them to some of mine. And, of course, there have been some tears, tantrums and arguments, but no more than you would get in any family. But, you see, I'd given up all hope of ever having a family. I had a hysterectomy for cancer ten years ago when I was twenty-five. I thought I would never be a mother. Jamie, Rob and Emma have been like a hundred years of Christmas and birthday presents all rolled into three little parcels, and I could never, ever have hoped for better than this.

Divorce and separation are adult solutions to adult problems, and remarriage is an adult choice. In a family the needs of the children are often paramount, but when the family breaks up and a new one forms, it is the adults' needs that come to the fore. Children can find this profoundly disturbing and their reactions and your expectations can lead to all sorts of complications. A reconstituted family will always produce situations that need to be addressed, but the result can be satisfying for all concerned if you are prepared to be aware of the potential problem areas and understand how they could affect everyone.

As a society we have not yet fully come to terms with other people's children. Even though step-relationships are now common and normal, we persist in seeing them as abnormal, deviant and somehow shameful. I hope that this book will help to counter that view, and there are two points I would like you to have recognized when you have read it. First, you are not alone and the blended family is just as common a type of family as any other, rather than a curiosity. Secondly, no family, blended or otherwise, is perfect and very few families have no problems. So, being a 'good enough' parent is the best you or your partner can realistically hope for under any circumstances. I would then like you to experience the relief that comes from realizing that the problems you face are likely to have arisen because of the situation rather than because you are uniquely inadequate or the children are uniquely wicked.

Michael, Cathy and Gordon are all members of blended families. The difficulties they are encountering seem to them to be peculiar to them and somehow their own fault. But many readers will recognize the situations and their stresses and strains as being somehow familiar. Why these have occurred, exactly what each member of a blended family might be feeling and what can be done about it are the themes we are going to explore in *Other People's Children*.

Michael's father, Marty, has been married to Sheila for a year and a half. Michael's mother and Sheila's husband both died suddenly and tragically, within days of each other. Sheila has three children – boys aged sixteen and six and a girl of nine. Michael is fifteen and has a twelve-year-old brother. The marriage and the family seem to be stabilizing, except for one element. Michael refuses to talk to Sheila and argues with his new stepbrothers and stepsister. Both Michael and his brother were sent back to boarding-school after their mother's death, but his brother has integrated into the family and has asked to stay at home and go to a day-school instead.

Holidays are hell. Michael complains of being ignored, but refuses to join in. He picks fights with the rest of the family, but insists that nobody is nice to him and generally creates an atmosphere. Sheila's mother has refused to have anything to do with her new step-grandchild since she sent him some presents at school and received no word of acknowledgement, let alone thanks. Marty's view is that if the boy wants to be a loner and refuses to become part of the new family, that is his choice and 'his lookout'.

Unlike Sheila, who feels it is important to remember her husband and discusses him and his death with the children, Marty refuses to talk about his dead wife. Perhaps this is because they were separated at the time of her death in a fire – and, according to him, she had a drink problem. As so often happens in these situations, nobody has asked Michael what he thinks. The son of an unhappy woman who may have given him a reason to be ambivalent towards her life and death, he was packed off to boarding-school immediately after the tragedy. Michael has good grounds for feeling guilty and unworthy. His every action is a challenge. He seems to be constantly saying, 'Am I really as unworthy, and dislikable as I think, and are you going to love me if I act badly?' The answer always appears to be, 'Yes, you are, and no, we won't.' His father has abandoned him for a new family, and even his younger brother has 'gone over' to the other side.

Cathy has an eleven-year-old son who, having lived with her ex-husband since their divorce ten years ago, recently moved in with her and her husband of four years. She has longed for this to happen and her husband was happy about it, but tension in the household has been increasing. As she says, 'Since he has been here, my husband has ignored him apart from when he has shouted at him or told him off, which is getting more frequent.' She cannot understand why this is so, as the boy did not appear suddenly, and the three of them used to spend perfectly happy weekends together when the boy was in his father's custody.

Cathy now feels she is a one-parent family because her husband will take no part in caring and will accept no responsibility for the boy. She says that he seems to think everything the boy does is wrong, and any attempts to discuss the situation become argumentative. While she loves her husband and cannot bear the thought of splitting up, she feels her loyalties towards her son must be greater than those to her husband.

Cathy's husband is both resentful and guilty about his feelings for the boy. He resents the child's presence because he is being expected to care for and love someone else's son. He resents the fact that Cathy's love and attention are now divided. Somehow, it would matter less if the cause of this was a child of his own. And he is guilty about being angry with and unfair to an innocent child. His emotions are so confused and contradictory that he believes he can cope only by blocking them out and refusing to discuss what is going on. He is rapidly coming to the conclusion that, after four years of happy marriage, the relationship he and Cathy had has changed for ever and for the worse, and it may be time to end it.

At the centre of this, and seen by all the adults concerned not as a thinking and caring human being but as a pawn and a symbol, is the boy. Sent away by one father who no longer wanted him and rejected by the new one, he is probably the most devastated. If he were being sullen, disobedient or obstreperous, it would be understandable. In fact, he is being over-eager to please and desperately engaging, but finding that even his best is not good enough.

Gordon is married to Valerie and they have a baby boy. Valerie also has three children by her ex-husband. Gordon tries valiantly to treat all the children as his own, but there is tension between him and the older ones, especially fourteen-year-old Lucy. Their father has recently turned up again, after ignoring them for nearly eight years. He has taken Lucy and her older brother, Mike, out and lavished gifts on them, but still takes no notice of his younger son, seven-year-old Thomas. According to Lucy, their new 'stepmum' is wonderful – the woman who made Valerie's life hell for two years with spiteful letters and abusive phone calls.

The ex-husband buys Mike and Lucy champagne, but contributes only £26 a month for the three children – a payment he has made for just the last few years. Valerie does not want to stop the children from seeing their father, but she needs to know how to deal with the anger that threatens to choke her every time her daughter praises her stepmother and abuses her stepfather. She needs to know how to cope with the fact that her ex-husband refuses even to acknowledge the existence of his youngest child. She needs to know how to praise and reward Gordon's patience, tolerance and kindness. Above all, she needs to know why her children and her ex-husband seem to conspire to make life so unbelievably complicated and unfair.

Outside Attitudes and Pressures

'Once upon a time a queen longed for a child. She wanted a daughter with skin as white as snow, lips red as blood and hair black as ebony. After years of waiting such a daughter was born and the Queen and the King called the girl Snow White. But before the child reached her second birthday, the Queen died. After a year had passed the King married again. The new Queen was beautiful, but proud and jealous. She had a magic looking-glass, and when she stood in front of it and said, "Looking-glass looking-glass on the wall, who is the fairest of them all?" the glass would answer, "You, oh Queen, are the fairest of them all." But the day came when it said, "You are the fairest here at hand, but Snow White is fairest in all the land." And from that day on the Queen schemed to do away with her stepdaughter.'

'There was once a merchant who had a beautiful, kind wife and a lovely daughter. The daughter was barely twelve years old when her mother died and after a year her father married again, to a woman with two daughters of her own. They were fair of face but black of heart, with tempers to match. Quarrels and heartache filled the home until the merchant's own daughter took refuge in the kitchen and became a scullery maid. Because they took away her silks and satins and forced her to sleep by the hearth in the ashes, they called her Cinderella.'

'A woodcutter lived in a great forest with his two children. Their mother had died when they were young and he had taken a second wife. They were so poor that their clothes were rags and they had very little to eat. One night the wife took her husband aside and said, "Tomorrow I want you to take the children into the forest until they are lost and leave them there. We can feed and clothe the two of us, but unless we get rid of the children, we shall all starve." Hansel and Gretel overheard their stepmother talking and set about making a plan to save themselves.'

Blended families have always had 'a bad press'. In a wide range of genres from fairy tales to the classics, from Shakespeare to present-day films, step-parents and step-siblings are common figures, but they are always the villains. Even if your parents never told you fairy stories, even if you have never read the classics and prefer soap opera to Shakespeare, you know that the word 'wicked' always goes in front of the word 'stepmother'. Stepfathers may be even worse. According to Hollywood, they are homicidal maniacs. Such images and stereotypes are part of our culture, and unless we are considering the subject closely for some reason, we tend to accept this picture. Step-parents are wicked, step-siblings are cruel and stepfamilies are out of the ordinary.

Why do we hold these views, and what effect have the myths on our ability to see what is actually going on? As I have already mentioned, restructured families are as old as any other family unit. They are not exactly a new phenomenon that we are still trying to fit into society and come to terms with. Jesus, strictly speaking, was brought up by a stepfather. From the time our ancestors 'pair bonded' – settled together in a partnership to give each other love and support and to raise children between them – new pairings must have been formed because of death or separation. And left over from the initial pairing there would have been children. Yet while we have unjustifiably optimistic images of a family life that proceeds along the 'normal' route through courtship, marriage and parenthood to dignified old age, we have only negative views if parenthood is followed by separation and a new cycle of courtship and marriage.

One reason for this may be that we make a sacred cow of a certain view of 'family'. There are strong pressures in our society to accept uncritically that a 'proper' family consists of two adults and their children living together in happiness and exclusivity. That is considered to be the norm and the optimum arrangement, giving comfort and stability to those within it. It may be a true picture of most families, but why does it cause unease and anger in so many of us even to suggest that other forms at least exist? It appears that to imply anything else is possible is to open up a frighteningly complex issue. Noticing just how many families give the lie to this image – and recognizing that such a large number of people, now and in the past, have experienced something different – may cause you to cast an anxious eye on your own family. We generally prefer to shy away from that exercise. The fear is that if other apparently happy families can be broken up by separation, divorce or death, the same thing could happen to us. So, we prefer not to talk about different forms of family. It is a kind of superstition – if we acknowledge they exist, we may allow such a disruption to happen to us. And, if we acknowledge that other, diverse forms of family – single-parent families, families made up of gay couples – may be happy too, we may conversely have to accept that what lies under the surface of an 'ordinary' family may not be so perfect after all.

How we approach a new partnership that will result in the restructuring of a family, possibly giving us another parent for our children and making us a parent for our partner's children, depends on two basic influences. The first is your own personal responses, which are often totally beyond your control and are set off by events in the past as much as by what occurs in the present. We will look at these in the next chapter. The second is the reaction of those around you – society at large, the community you live in, your family and your friends. We do not live in a vacuum and, whether we realize it or not, the beliefs held by those around us profoundly affect the way we feel, act and behave. To understand what may happen when a restructured family comes together, we need to consider how outside pressures may alter our expectations of step-parenting, and how we perform the role.

External influence can take various forms. You, a partner and your children may be affected by the beliefs and assumptions of people you know or meet concerning what is happening specifically to you, in your home; and all of you may be affected by wider beliefs and assumptions, held by society as a whole about blended families as a whole. There are a few fairly common examples of the first. When forming a family unit where there are children from a previous relationship, many couples find that friends and family feel that the adult 'taking on' someone else's children is doing the parent and children a favour. If you operate on the assumption that everyone else ought to be grateful merely for accepting that part of the package, you may find it hard to acknowledge and come to terms with the resentments, angers and split loyalties that sometimes ensue.

When Rosemary married her second husband, Alec, she encountered this attitude, particularly from Alec himself and his family. Her two sons, Joe and Barry, by a previous husband, found it a strain. The second relationship lasted five years but ended in divorce three years ago.

When I look back on it, the relationship with my second husband was always difficult. I think part of the reason was that my eldest took against him from

21

the word go. Alec came into the relationship with rather the feeling that he was doing the kids a favour, and his mother never let us forget it. Joe's favourite refrain at that time was, 'Don't think he's going to get any thanks from me.' And frankly, if Alec had saved his life, Joe would probably have turned his back on him. Perhaps it would have worked if there hadn't been this feeling all the time that we should only count our blessings and not look a gift-horse in the mouth. But Joe just wasn't allowed to say what was bothering him, and when Alec and I started having problems, neither was I. The whole attitude was that we should be thankful just for having this man around the house and not get involved in petty complaints like the fact that he was a bully and never listened to anything we said.

Martin found this idea of doing favours equally irritating, mainly because, as the partner joining the family, he thinks that he is gaining the most. He had known Jenny for fifteen years when her first marriage ended; they had been neighbours and at the same school when teenagers. He had always fancied her, but had been too shy to ask for a date when they were young. As a successful manager in a large firm, he felt confident enough to approach her with more than just friendship in mind as soon as he heard of her divorce. They have been married just under a year and have two children from her previous marriage, with no plans at present to add to their family.

The patronizing attitude of a lot of my friends and family just about sends me up the wall. I overheard someone at work once talking about me and making out like I was some incredible saint who had taken on this secondhand woman and her bratty little kids out of the goodness of my heart. I just wanted to scream at him, 'For God's sake, I love Jenny. The sex is great, the children are fabulous. I don't want gratitude, it isn't *about* gratitude. I'm perfectly happy with the situation.' Even her mother introduces me round at family gatherings with this sort of eyebrow-raised 'Would you believe it?' air and I swear to God that if we ever had a bad argument, even if I hit her around, most of her friends and family would tell her that she should put up with anything from me and be grateful. *I'm* the one who should be grateful, but you try getting them to understand that.

In society as a whole there are quite rigidly held views about who should marry whom. Marriage between people of a different race, class or educational attainment, for instance, may come under scrutiny from friends and family. When a single person marries someone who has already been married and has a family, this concept of crossing the line of acceptable behaviour can also come into play. The spoken or unspoken criticism is that one partner is not doing as well as he or she might and the other is unfairly getting somebody of a higher status than they deserve.

When Carol and Philip met fifteen years ago, she was a single woman in her early twenties and he a divorced man in his forties with four children. While she did not have any problem with her contemporaries, she thinks that

there is a general negative view which is very unhelpful. It seems to say, 'If you are a successful person, why didn't you marry someone of your own age and have your own children?' I used to hear that I was an attractive single woman, so why did I bodge it up by marrying an older man with all those responsibilities? This attitude is far more prevalent than you think.

There can be enormous hostility if the new partner is thought to be the cause of a separation or divorce, as Kirsty and Stan found. Eight years ago he left his previous wife and two children to live with her, and they married two years later, when his divorce was finalized. Kirsty and Stan have a good relationship with her family, but since his separation he has not been able to have any friendly contact with his ex-wife and children or his children's grandparents, or even with his own parents. Kirsty explains:

> Their marriage was over before I met Stan, but they were still living together. So you'll find his children still, to this day, say that I bust up the happy home. I'm the villain of the piece, the Jezebel who stole their weak father away from their loving mother. Well, it stands to reason, doesn't it? I'm ten years younger than she is, so I must be a slut. Even his own mother agrees, and she's hardly spoken a word to him in the six years we've been married. She sees his ex all the time, though.

This hostility may be just as great if the new partner is younger, more attractive or better off than the previous partner, or is seen to be taking too soon the place of someone who has died.

Many people are made to feel isolated or shunned both when a family breaks up and when it re-forms. You may find, or already have found, that while you are single, most of your friends are in the same state. Once you get married or are living with someone, your friends are also couples. This is either because all of you are at an age when you are going through similar stages in life, or because you gravitate towards other people in the same position. Married couples or long-term partners, especially those with children, seldom have single friends. This could be because people have less in common if they do not share the same concerns of married life and parenthood. Another explanation is that one member in a couple may feel threatened by a singleton. Couples can find the single state alarming and even fear that it is a 'catching' condition. The member of the couple who is the same sex as the single friend may be tempted to copy him or her and become a free agent again, while the one of the opposite sex may be tempted to have an affair.

So, when a relationship changes following separation, divorce or death, you may find that old friends, even best friends, abandon you or cool off. This is not just because they are thinking of themselves and their own relationships. We often avoid someone who is going or has gone through a difficult or depressing time because we do not feel able to help and may even make things worse. We think it would look silly not to mention what has happened, but that if we do talk about it, the tears will start. We then feel guilty at having upset a friend and do not know what to say.

Val endured a period of isolation after her husband, Steve, asked for a trial separation and moved out last year. Three weeks after leaving he confessed to her that he had no intention of coming back and was, in fact, living with someone else.

I seemed to lose a lot of friends when Steve and I broke up. I was so wrapped up in my own misery at first that I didn't notice that the phone had stopped ringing. But after a few weeks it became pretty obvious. I'd meet people I knew in the street or in the supermarket and they always had something very urgent they were hurrying to get to. It really sank home, though, when I invited my best friend and her husband over for a meal and they cancelled at the last moment. When I tried to make another date, she was evasive. I finally tackled

25

her about it and she said it wasn't her choice, but her husband just didn't want to see me at the moment. I don't know what he was scared of, but that was the impression I got – he was scared.

When you start a new relationship that may be seen as 'normal' in that you are once more part of a couple, everyone may have a vested interest in its being as normal as possible. Enormous pressure may be put on all those concerned for it to be so. The hope is that the new couple and any children will have found a 'happily ever after', and will join the former social circle again. If the actual situation does not go quite by the anticipated script, we may try to force what is going on into that acceptable mould, resulting in misery. Friends and relatives may ignore all the signs or even argue you out of reservations if you try to express them. Some or all of those involved may then think they have to pretend to their friends or people outside the home that the relationships within are happy. The pretence may not be only for other people's benefit. We may try to fool ourselves too and insist that all is well when we know that there are some problems that have not been tackled. Mark, for instance, found his mother quite unable to voice her misgivings about how he might feel towards her new partner. His parents split up when he was three and his father lost contact soon after. His mother decided to remarry when he was thirteen.

I think she had known him for some time. He was sort of around for a bit, but I can't say I'd really noticed him much. Then she brought him home one afternoon and summonsed me into the living-room and introduced us, which I thought was really weird. And then, of course, he drops the bombshell that they're getting married. I can't remember that I said much, but I got away after ten minutes or so and went to my room. When he'd gone, she came in and started walking around picking up my things and rearranging stuff – you know, like mothers do, and it always drives you crazy. She went on about how much he liked me and how glad she was that it was all right by me and that I liked him too. But I hadn't said a thing about what I thought about him. I certainly hadn't said that I liked him. I know I hadn't said that, and that I'd never done anything to give her the idea that I thought that. Although I didn't have much against him, I wasn't exactly happy at the idea that he could waltz in and take over just like that. What really got up my nose was the fact that she went on and on and stopped me ever having the chance of saying what I really thought. I don't think she wanted to hear any different – she sure as hell never gave me a chance to say it.

Having a strong belief and aspirations about how we would like a family to be is not harmful in itself. The problems come when we set up fantasies and insist that they rule our lives and actions, even when such insistence begins to create difficulties. There are two contradictory myths that hinder making good relationships in a blended family. The first is that everything in the garden is lovely. If this is your second partnership, when you tell friends and relatives that you are remarrying, you may find yourself the subject of a sustained campaign of gooey sentimentality. 'How wonderful – the children will have a father/mother again, and what a relief for you.' Steph felt tremendous pressure to look on the bright side when her second marriage was mooted. She and her first husband had divorced after eight years of marriage, leaving her alone with two children:

He went back to the States and as far as I know has a

new family – he certainly hasn't made any effort to keep in touch with the old one. My friends were delighted when I said I was getting married again. A new man for me and a new father for Beth and Brian was all they could see. I knew it wasn't as simple as that, but whenever I tried to bring this up, I'd get hushed and shushed.

People do not live happily ever after, without a degree of planning, effort and, most important, awareness and insight. If you are going to take on the emotion-laden task of making a new family out of the ashes of an old one, the first requirement is that you at least acknowledge what you are doing. The chances are, however, that any reservations on your or your partner's part may be ignored, drowned out or pushed aside, which will not make your lives any easier. If this is your first partnership and you are the one to acquire a ready-made family, people will say, 'Oh, won't that be fun. You can miss out on the nappies and go straight to the enjoyable bits!' We often cling, desperately, to this kind of belief simply *because* we suspect that the second myth is the truth – the myth that says a step-relationship cannot ever work, that step-parents and stepchildren will be unable to love each other, will find it difficult to tolerate each other or will end up hating each other. As one stepfather said, 'He's not my own blood. How can you be expected to love a kid who's not your own?' Adam met just this reaction when his father's second marriage was announced.

I never really knew my mum, she died when I was very young. But I felt I'd known her because my father talked about her a lot. He had girlfriends when I was little, and I always wanted him to bring me a mum. He didn't bring many girlfriends home. I think it was because he knew none of them were going to last and he didn't want to upset me. But Molly was different. After a time she moved in, and then they said they were going to get married. I was just over the moon and thought it was great that I was going to get a real mum at last. It was a right slap in the face when I told my friends and they all said, 'God that's awful.' Even my best friend's mum said, 'Poor you', as if it was going to be bad. My teacher called me in on my own and told me that if I had any problems, I could come and talk to him. Everyone seemed to think it was bad news. I got quite paranoid and started wondering if they all knew something I didn't know. Molly was brill – total genius. She saw that I had gone all moody and she came into my room one night with a pile of books and sat down and started reading them aloud. What she had was all these fairy stories that were about stepmothers. When she got to about the fifth one, we were both in fits of giggles and she said, 'Was that what they told you I'd be like?' and I said, 'Yeah', and it ended up a big joke. I introduce her now as my Wicked Stepmother, and when I give her a card, like at Christmas or on her birthday, I send it to 'The WSM'. My original mum would have liked her. I certainly do.

Why should it be so difficult to love someone who is not your own blood? There may be personal differences, of course; an adult and a child who have not grown up together may clash, just as two adults can. To answer this question we need to look at how instinctive patterns of behaviour make us see someone who is not related to us and not chosen by us as an alien, an invader and even an enemy.

We know that how we live and how we feel are based on social patterns that come from the human race's drive to ensure survival. Sometimes the survival of the species as a whole is gained at the expense of individual members. A living being, whether human, antelope or tiger, is impelled to try to preserve and further its own genes – the genetic blueprint that is taken from your cells and repeated in your offspring. In animals that live in groups, feed on grass or other vegetation and are prey to meat-eating animals, selfishness and exclusivity are survival traits. Survival of your own progeny often relies on throwing someone else's to the wolves. If the herd is surrounded by hungry flesh-eaters, fit animals will make a run for it, leaving the halt and the lame to be taken to give themselves a chance to get free. None stops to help, and none would look after an orphaned or abandoned youngster. As any farmer can tell you, if a foster parent is needed for a young calf or lamb, the farmer has to go to extraordinary lengths to fool the foster mother into believing the youngster is her own. So, it would seem that having no empathy for and, indeed, feeling positively hostile towards a child who does not bear your own genes is a natural state of affairs that we cannot hope to change.

But caring for their own offspring alone is not the sole type of social behaviour found in the animal world. Pack animals tend to follow a different pattern from herd animals. In a group of wolves or big cats, for example, all the members pool their resources and help bring up the young. Lionesses suckle cubs in their pride indiscriminately, whether they are their own or those of a sister lioness. Admittedly, often only certain members are allowed to breed – the top male and his mate or the top females – and most members of such a group are related. It could be argued that by looking after your sister's or your cousin's child you further your genes as much as if you looked after your own. But it proves that in nature not all animals demand that the young must be strictly their own before they will parent them.

What humans have in addition to our animal inheritance is the ability to think and act on more than instinct. In an age when we are realizing that the whole world is an extended community – the so-called 'global village' – is it too much to expect us also to see that the inhabitants are nothing but an extended family?

Part of the isolation and guilt endured by many adults involved with other people's children arises from the rigid, simple definition that is usually applied to what is a vague and complex situation. We tend to feel easier if we can slot people, and ourselves, into the right, neatly labelled pigeon-hole. If you marry a man or woman and his or her child lives permanently with you, clearly you are a step-parent, the child is a stepchild and you all form a stepfamily. But many who have contact with someone else's child, and the children themselves, are not in such a clear-cut position. You may be a weekend and holiday parent whom the children visit only for short periods; the children and the adult with whom they live most of the time may resent the idea of your taking on any 'parental' responsibilities at all. You may, having been once bitten, decide not to validate a permanent relationship by getting married. Everyone may then find it difficult to describe their places in the family. You yourselves may not even have a clear picture of where you fit in.

Such relationships can be intricate and confusing. Reconstituted families comprise an enormous range of relationships, all of which give rise to varying degrees of contact between adults and children even if you or your partner is being denied access to the children by the parent who looks after them full time. Whether you are married, living with your partner without having gone through a ceremony or seeing your partner on a regular basis, and whether you are one of the parents or the non-related adult, you and any children are likely to be affected by the complicated circumstances that surround relationships of this sort, whatever the level of actual contact. All the following people are in new extended or reconstituted families, though some of them have found that they have been denied status by others and are not considered to be members of a 'real stepfamily'.

Carol and Philip married nine years ago and have two children of their own, aged eight and four. Philip had four children from his previous marriage who lived with their mother and are now all grown up. Three of them lived with Carol and Philip at various times.

Marvin is twenty-one. His parents separated when he was eleven and he stayed with his mother. His father moved in with a girlfriend whom he married four years later, and she is now expecting a baby. His mother has been living with a former boyfriend for the last eight years.

Anna and John met ten years ago and lived together for three years before marrying. She had separated from her husband two years before meeting John. Her son, Nigel, lives with his father. Periodically Nigel visits John and Anna, who now have three of their own children. Nigel's father has remarried and in that family Nigel has a stepsister and a further two half-brothers.

Julia is seventeen, and her parents separated when she was ten. Her father remarried and her mother has a permanent partner. The two families live within half a mile of each other. Julia has a bedroom in both houses and splits her time evenly between them. Her younger sister lives mostly with their mother and spends only the odd night with their father. Her father and his second wife, Joy, have a five-year-old daughter and a two-year-old son, and Joy has an eight-year-old son by her previous marriage who sometimes stays with his father and his new family. Julia's mother and partner, Steve, have a three-year-old daughter and are expecting another baby.

Mike and Alison have lived together for four years. She and her husband have been separated for six years but since they are Catholic cannot be divorced. Her two sons by that marriage are at boarding-school and spend alternate holidays with each parent. Their father also has a new relationship.

Jack is seventeen and an only child. His parents separated when he was seven and his father has since remarried. Jack lives with mother and her partner of ten years. Both Jack's parents are in their fifties; his mother's partner is sixty-six and his stepmother is in her late thirties. His mother's partner has a son whom Jack has hardly met.

Deirdre and James have lived together for eighteen years. James's son, Paul, now twenty-six, lived with and was brought up by his mother, Laura. He stayed with Deirdre and James during holidays and occasionally at weekends.

Moira, who is fifteen, lives with her mother, Jane, brother, Roy, and stepfather, Adrian. Adrian and Jane have one daughter, Rachel, who is eighteen months old. Moira's older brother, Steven, lives with their father, and Adrian's son, Ian, lives away from home. Both Ian and Steven refuse to visit the new family.

Caroline has three children and is separated from her husband, who lives with his new partner. He maintains a strong link with the two younger ones, both boys, but will have nothing to do with the older child, a teenage girl. She in turn is extremely hostile to any man Caroline brings into the house and is doing her best to discourage Caroline's new boyfriend, Tony, who would very much like to become a permanent member of the family.

Jenny left her husband, Ben, and two children three years ago to live with Tom. Ben has stopped her from seeing them ever since, and in spite of her efforts she has been unable to re-establish contact. Tom also has a child by a previous relationship, but he no longer tries to keep up that link.

The fact that the relationship between many members of

a new extended family is denied a title in this society does not mean that it has no existence. Deirdre, for instance, who has known Paul, her partner James's son, for nineteen years, feels that

> he *is* a son to me. After James, I've made him my next of kin and if, God forbid, anything should happen to James, my relationship with Paul would remain. We may not be linked by blood or marriage, but we *are* linked. But this is very hard for other people to recognize and sometimes I even feel the need to apologize for it or explain it to people. For a long time I didn't tell Paul himself how I felt because I wasn't sure how he felt about it. It's as if I was trying to be possessive about him by just having these feelings when I had absolutely no right to be like that. I was rather nervous that he or anyone else was going to turn round to me and say, 'Who the hell do you think you are? You've got no call on him at all.'

To understand what pressures society puts on us in a new blended family, we have to understand how step-parents are usually expected to behave. The common idea is that step-parents move in and assume the position of a parent. That is, they are expected to love and care for, discipline and provide for children who are thenceforth seen as their offspring – which, of course, is where so much of the trouble starts. A new partner may smoothly replace the old one in the adult's eyes, but as far as a child is concerned (as we will discuss fully in Chapter 5), a parent is your parent for life. The new partner can indeed become a highly significant adult in the child's life, but in many cases he or she cannot take over the role of the parent, even if this man or woman was or still is a monster who is feared and hated by the child, and it is a mistake to try to do so.

Parenting is a complex package of feelings and behaviour that is difficult to pin down. A parent does more than feed, clothe and house his or her offspring, and more than 'love them'. A parent cares for children, not just in providing, but also in worrying about and feeling responsible for what the child does and experiences. A parent gives trust and unconditional love, love that continues even if the child is naughty, wayward or bad. Men and women sometimes find it hard to supply all that for the children they have given birth to, and part of being a parent is disliking the things your children do, feeling angry, upset, fed up and bored with them and sometimes not wanting to have them around.

There is an enormous contradiction in these expectations – you must take on the role of parent but at the same time you will never be able to have the same feelings. A stepfather or stepmother is expected to walk in and take on the mantle of the missing parent, perform this function flawlessly and love the child. If this is not done, they may be criticized and they will certainly feel guilty at being inadequate. But how can we expect people to accept and love children who are not of their bodies if at the same time our society places so much emphasis on 'your own' and insists that it is simply not possible to feel love for another person's child? Many find it hard to envisage caring for someone else's child, or parents that are not related by blood, even when the relationship is formed by express intention. Penny and Chris adopted their two children, Helen and Thomas, when they were babies. Penny has learned that

> some people do find it strange – if you haven't given birth to a child yourself, then how can you love it as much?

And one response Helen has had is:

35

'How awful for you.' I ask them what's so awful about it and they say, 'It's not your *real* mum and dad.'

If these views are held when a child has been specifically chosen to become part of a family, it is easy to see how reservations may be stronger, and more strongly voiced, when children arrive as part of the 'package deal' of a re-marriage.

Besides being evident in the expectations and assumptions of friends or family, society's attitudes towards blended families come across in more concrete terms. That our society fails to recognize the validity of the links between the individuals in a re-formed family is shown by the fact that the step-relationship has no standing at all in law. This might seem understandable in a case, for instance, where a couple were living together without formalizing their relationship with marriage. You might expect the partner to have no status in law, even if a child is living with the couple. And there is obviously a difficulty in formalizing the status between children and a parent's new partner if the children remain with the other parent. British law at present goes still further, however. No legal relationship exists between a child and his or her parent's new partner even when the couple are married and the children live with them permanently.

To an extent this is a necessary and correct acknowledgement of the importance of the continuing ties between children and their birth parents. If a legal and binding connection between a child and the new adult is made, the tie between the child and the absent birth parent is weakened. (The reasons for maintaining this tie are discussed in Chapter 5.) But the origin of such a law does not lie in an understanding of, or care for, the child's needs. It is an expression of our society's views on parenthood. Animals might reject another creature's offspring out of an instinctive need to preserve their own genes at the cost of others. In a sense we do the same in our law by allowing for the acknowledgement of only our own issue and not accepting someone else's.

Some members of a re-formed family may consider this an advantage. An adult living with a partner's children has no legal or financial obligations towards them. The new Child Support Act, which came into force in April 1993, does not apply to step-parents. Marrying someone who has children gives you absolutely no responsibilities for those children. Of course, this also means you have absolutely no rights over them either. The combination of responsibilities without rights is often at the root of the difficulties experienced by all members of restructured families.

Many adults in this situation are in fact happy to become responsible for a partner's children. You may feel that you and they form a family. Indeed, as far as the Census takers are concerned you do, even though the law makes no allowance for binding ties, as Sylvia found out to her and 'her' children's extreme cost.

I married Hugh in 1985 when Sam and Josh were five and six. Their mother had left them the previous year and gone off with another man. We had a tough time at first because she kept coming back in fits and starts, basically whenever her relationship was going badly. This made the kids very unsettled. Then we had a long period when we didn't hear from her and they settled down. During Christmas 1989 Hugh was killed in a car crash, and three months later she reappeared and asked for the kids. I couldn't believe it and told her to get the hell out. The next thing I knew she was at the door with a solicitor. I didn't have a legal leg to stand on apparently, because it had never occurred to Hugh and me to put anything in writing or have me adopt them. We just never thought it was necessary. I haven't seen them for a year now, and she's moved house. I don't know what sort of state they are in and I don't know if they will ever forgive me for letting them go. It could even have been what they wanted. I simply don't know.

Until the passing of the Children Act in 1989 children whose parents were divorcing or separating were considered to be the property of their parents. If custody of the children, or care and control and access to them, was fought over in the courts, it was probably with the parents' views of what was right and necessary uppermost. The Children Act changed the emphasis so that what is most important now is not what the parents want but what is right for the children. We no longer accept parents' rights to fight about ownership or access to children, but are trying to enforce each child's right to have access to both parents. For this reason, in the place of concepts such as custody and access – which see the situation from the parents' point of view – we have new terms: parental responsibility, residence orders and contact orders.

Step-parents can formalize their legal relationships with children by adopting them or by applying for a residence order under Section 8 of the Children Act. Adoption makes children your own, to all intents and purposes. You then have full responsibility for them and full parental rights over them, even if the birth parent to whom you are married dies. The only difference between you and a birth parent as far as the law is concerned is that you did not give birth to the child. It has to be stressed that adoption by step-parents is not very common, and will be allowed only if the circumstances are exceptional and there is no better way of giving the child the stability needed. A residence order puts you *in loco parentis* – in the place of a parent. While the children are in your care, you act as a parent and have responsibilities for and some rights over them, but they are not acknowledged as your children in law. Since English law follows marriage and blood lines, a stepchild cannot inherit from a step-parent unless he or she is named in a will or has been adopted by the step-parent. It is necessary to ask the court for permission to change a child's surname. If they have not been adopted, stepchildren can take on the surname of their step-parent only with the consent of both birth parents.

A step-parent can obtain a residence order by applying through the courts with the agreement of both birth parents, though this permission is not required if he or she has lived with the child for three years. A residence order gives parental responsibility until a stepchild is sixteen years, and it can be extended to eighteen years. You are likely to obtain an order only if it is deemed better than the option of not having one at all. In the awarding of both residence orders and adoption the first consideration is the best interests of the child. The problem is, however, that what is best for the child is not always best for the parents. The uncertainty and anxiety of parents and step-parents who feel their position is insecure may make things worse for everyone concerned.

If the law finds it difficult to accept and therefore define the wide range of bonds that exist between adults and other people's children, the institutions in our society find it even harder. Couples such as Christine and Gregory have struggled when filling in forms that ask for details of family and offspring. They met seven years ago and have been married for three years. His three children from a previous marriage stay with them every other weekend, and they have two children of their own. Christine remembers trying to explain the situation when buying their house together.

> We had to fill in a mortgage form and answer questions like 'How many children do you have?' What is the answer? So I said, 'Five', and there was this look of terror across the face of the interviewer who said, 'Five', looking at me as if to say you can't have five. So I said, 'Three stepchildren and two of my own.' But there wasn't space for this on the form so she wrote two. I thought, No, this isn't right. We're moving into a four-bedroomed house because we have five children, not because we have two.

Deirdre and James, who have been living together for many years, find the same problem. James has a son, Paul, by a previous marriage.

> Forms are totally infuriating. It's bad enough that they insist that the only relationship between two people can be marriage – being a partner or living together is just not allowed for. But Paul simply doesn't exist as far as they are concerned. You are asked about dependants, but since he doesn't live with us he doesn't count. James didn't contribute regular maintenance for him – at the time of the split between him and Laura he gave a lump sum basically by giving her the proceeds of the sale of the house and all the contents. When Paul used to stay with us, James would contribute towards clothes and that sort of thing. But we were contributing, and I say 'we' because the money came out of our joint budget and at times it was a strain. So the fact that there was no space on any form to fill in 'sort of semi-dependant who certainly costs us something' irritated the hell out of me. He's a next of kin to us both after each other, but again that doesn't count, does it?

Given that a large number of children in this society live in blended families – in a recent study in a class of nine-year-olds 79 per cent were found to be living in one – it is extraordinary that many schools tend to be unable to accept the reality of reconstituted families. Most now appear to have some guidelines in dealing with and being aware of the existence of one-parent families, and many teachers have been trained not to assume that every child has two parents. But there seems to have been no recognition of the need to understand the complex dynamics of two-parent families where one of the adults may not be related directly to the child in question or one-parent families where not only the non-custodial father but also his new partner are keenly involved in the upbringing and well-being of the child.

Deirdre can remember visiting Paul's primary school on an open night and walking around with him while Laura and James spoke to his teacher.

We met the headteacher, who immediately assumed since I was an adult and with Paul that I must be his mother. He breezily introduced himself and was obviously totally nonplussed when Paul corrected him by saying, 'No, this isn't my mother. It's my father's flatmate.'

'Flatmate' was his current euphemism for it, but I know that changed at various times during our long and happy relationship. What I certainly never was was a stepmother, and he would have resisted fiercely any suggestion of mother status because he had one perfectly good mother of his own and didn't need another.

It may be understandable that schools and teachers are unprepared or caught off guard when faced with the complications of a blended family. It is not so easy to be forgiving when, as so frequently happens, official ignorance is converted into open pressure. Paul found that some of the teachers in his school were not prepared to acknowledge his happy acceptance of his situation:

I know an awful lot of people of my age whose parents are separated, remarried and so on. Because of this it has always been irritating to me that a great deal of your time at school is spent explaining to everyone that, for example, your father and mother probably won't be or can't attend parents' evening together because they live separate lives. And that this woman you are with is ... what? Your stepmother, your father's girlfriend (unsuitable for any 18 + relationship, really), partner? Some stepfamily relationships run into problems, identity crises and the need to find new rules and definitions of what's what. This process is very important to those involved because that is what makes it work. The last thing you need is people who cannot deal with what is now a very common phenomenon (often because it would involve making admissions about their own lives) or try to put a name to it for you. 'Not Deirdre,' a teacher once said to me at junior school, '*Aunty* Deirdre.' As if, not being my real mother or my father's real wife, I wasn't expected to be on first-name terms with her.

The effect of external beliefs and pressure, of the attitudes and behaviour of the wider family network, cannot be underestimated. As you can see, plenty of myths are current in society and there is much misunderstanding about reformed families. This inevitably results in pressures, some of which are easy to recognize and contain. Second marriages are one and a half to twice as likely to end in divorce as first marriages, and the presence of children from another partnership is probably a contributory factor. Children are reported to be the second most frequent subject fuelling a row in remarriages. The most frequent is money – and that may well relate to stepchildren too.

It is often said that when a couple make love in the privacy of their own bedroom, there are actually six people present: the couple themselves and, in spirit, both sets of parents. When you go to bed with a new partner and one or both of you has children from a previous relationship, the chances are that your ex-partners, their parents and all of your children are also part of that invisible, critical and daunting audience. And not just in bed. In the kitchen, bathroom and living-room you are under scrutiny and up for judgement. Both the adults and the children in step-relationships find they are quick to heap anger, hatred and blame on the other. It is easy to see how difficulties may be inherent in restructured families. But what are the effects of these on the adults and children involved? In the next chapter we will be looking at many of the problems encountered in blended families and considering what sort of situations you may experience.

3
What Are the Problems?

'The problems weren't really the things I'd expected. I'd thought we'd have arguments between my kids and his and there would be jealousies and bickering. But it was me and his oldest daughter who really had the main trouble and that took me by surprise. I put it down to her being a little madam, always wanting her own way. It took my own best friend to point out that I was a bit hard on her and might be jealous myself, her being a pretty teenager with a way with her dad. I hadn't thought of that, but I think it was true.'

What are the problems that might confront you as a member of a blended family? The way your family is constructed may be relevant – how many children, their ages and their approach to the new situation. Practical concerns such as money, housing and day-to-day routines ought to be considered too. Recognizing a problem and that it may be an understandable reaction to a situation is often a first step to doing something about it.

The most important aspects of all are probably the very reasons for your being where you are: part of a couple where for at least one of you it is the second time around. It is hardly surprising that a reconstituted family comes across difficulties. Even in the happiest first-time relationships nobody starts with a completely clean sheet. There may have been earlier boyfriends or girlfriends and there may also have been events in your childhood or teenage years that affect your ability to make a happy and lasting relationship. But second-time families have all this as well as the after-effects not only of the first relationship but of its ending. After all, the main precipitating factor behind the formation of a blended family is divorce. In other words, most reconstituted families come together in the shadow of a breakdown in a former relationship, and alongside the living presence of the former partner. This is probably why families in which the man was previously married are twice as likely to end in divorce as families where both are first-timers, and one and a half times as likely to do so where the woman was previously married.

Divorce may be the end of a marriage, but very rarely is the break clean and complete. Feelings of failure, anger and resentment, and the overwhelming desire to express these and have the other partner recognize them, often result in a continuing battle. This often goes on for an extraordinarily long time after the formal end of the relationship. Carol and Philip have been married for nine years and have regular contact with the four children of his previous marriage. Carol says that his ex-wife has

> remained sad, bitter and angry and I don't know how much I could get on with her or how much she'd want it. Even if I did get on with her, the crucial bit is, I think, Philip, her and the children. I've tended to stay away, but we have met.

Even though a couple have parted, there is often unfinished business between them. Both may consider that the other has not even acknowledged, let alone heard or understood, their emotions. Because of this sense of not yet having drawn a line and ended the relationship, many continue to feel connected in some way to their former partner. This can happen when a couple part and there are no children to provide a tangible link or proof that there was once something between them. It has to be even more likely when they are both still parents to their child or children. Children form an invisible chain tying the two adults together. They may also provide a conduit through which arguments are channelled.

Richard and Ellen divorced twenty years ago when their two children were two and three. Richard has maintained contact with the children, though this has not always been easy.

She got at me for years afterwards through the kids. Petty little arguments like not having them ready in time when I went to collect them, but then raising a fuss if I got them back late by so much as a minute. I know, because they started to report it to me as they got a bit older, that it was always 'Your father doesn't really care for you' or 'He's only doing this to get at me.' It got far worse when I married Carrie, and for a time got a bit better when she remarried too. But the weird thing was that through all of this, and, let's face it, we divorced over twenty years ago, she has never really broken off some sort of contact with me. It's as if we hadn't got divorced but I'd run off with someone else and would be coming back sometime. In her eyes it was almost as if I was out on temporary loan. I see myself as the father of these kids and a co-parent with her of them. I simply don't see myself any more as anything to do with her, and I haven't done for, oh, it must be ten or fifteen years now. But she *still* sees me as her estranged husband and I think she always will. Our kids are grown up now and there is very little reason for us to have any contact at all, but I know she still expects it. I may have the piece of paper to prove I divorced her, but the truth of the matter is that she has never divorced me.

When a new partner and a chance for a new family come along, it may none the less be very difficult to break away from the memories or the patterns of the old one. This is equally true if you chose to leave the old relationship or were glad that it ended as if you were the one who was abandoned. Whatever the reason for your now starting in a new relationship, memories, habits and comparisons with the old one may intrude. Andrea feels that her partner, and his children, constantly compare her with his ex-wife. He moved in when his wife discovered he had been having an affair with Andrea for two years, and they have now been together for two and a half years.

Bill has never said anything, but I always feel that he is forever comparing me with Jane. The kids are far less tongue-tied. Whenever they come to stay, they make it quite clear that the food I serve them, the decoration in the house and the clothes I wear, even the things I'm interested in or say, are just the lowest of the low compared with what their beautiful, wonderful and talented mother has.

So, however much you may think or hope that a second marriage or partnership may be a new start, you need to recognize that it is impossible to sweep away the influences of what has gone before.

Divorce or separation is, after death, the second most stressful life event to occur in a family. Indeed, studies have shown that children who have lost a parent through death often cope far better with the immediate and long-term aftermath than those who have lost a parent through divorce or separation. Becky's father died ten years ago when she was fifteen after a long illness.

My best friend was really quite amazing. She came over as soon as she heard and stayed with me up until the funeral. She knew how I was feeling because the week before this happened she'd also lost her father, but he hadn't died. He left to live with someone who had been a family friend. When I look back on how both of us were feeling at the time and during the following year, I am struck by the fact that it was so much easier for me to get over it all. It was all very focused. He died, we were unhappy, we cried and everyone gave us sympathy and then we gradually got over it. You never get over it in one way, because you always miss your father when he's gone, but at least he was gone and we knew where we were. With her it was never really over. He still lives quite near by and she keeps having to cope with the same feelings over and over again, even though she herself is now married.

When a partnership ends in death, you are left to grieve. When it ends in divorce or separation, grief is complicated because everyone concerned cannot help but fear that it was somehow their fault. It is a common belief that if something goes wrong, somebody must be 'to blame'. Many of us grow up with a nagging feeling that it is we who are lacking, for young people tend to think that their parents are faultless and that they themselves are always the culprits. When we believe in our heart of hearts that we are in the wrong, it is a very human reaction to point the finger at someone else. The break-up of a family is a sad event, but it is often made into a particularly difficult tragedy by the amount of mutual anger and accusation that so often surrounds it.

The degree of grief and the cocktail of accompanying emotions are uncannily similar whether the death is of a person or of a relationship. Feelings of shock, disbelief and self-pity are all to be expected. The other two likely reactions, anger and guilt, are definitely harder to come to terms with. Anger is often turned inward, in self-destructive disgust, and it can become physical; you can feel cold and shivery and also that everything is rather 'unreal'.

An American study of the early 1980s found that three features increased the chances of a poor outcome for the surviving partner, each of which leads to a particular 'grief syndrome'. All three syndromes are just as applicable to the survivors of relationships that have ended as they are to those who are trying to cope with death.

The first syndrome occurred when the death was sudden and unexpected. The people here

- had difficulty in believing in the full reality of the loss and avoided confronting it
- were more likely in early weeks to show deeper distress and anxiety and have feelings of self-reproach and despair
- as time passed, had a sense of social withdrawal
- had a sense of the continued presence of the lost partner
- had a continuing sense of loneliness, anxiety and depression

Only 9 per cent of the people in this category were rated as having a good outcome a year later, compared with 56 per cent of those who had long been expecting the death.

The second syndrome was evident in those who had had an argumentative relationship with the late partner and were not sure whether they really regretted the loss, causing a reaction of anger and self-reproach. These people showed:

- low levels of initial distress, later followed by more severe grief
- continued yearning for the return of the lost partner
- continued high level of guilt and anxiety
- in the long term, signs of depression and a general deterioration of health
- a lack of confidence over performance at work or as a parent

Of this group 29 per cent had a good outcome after a year, compared with the 61 per cent who had had better relationships.

The third syndrome was intense yearning after the death, and was most common when a person had been so dependent on the former partner that he or she was unable to perform the ordinary tasks of life without the partner's help. The distinctive features were at first:

- feelings of insecurity, emptiness and loneliness
- a sense of unreality
- a strong sense of the continuing presence of the late partner

and later

- a continued high level of yearning for, and sense of presence of, the lost partner
- a propensity to complain of loneliness and to say, 'Deep down I wouldn't care if I died tomorrow'

Difficulties in adjusting to the ending of a relationship are increased because at present our legal system turns couples who are divorcing into adversaries. Instead of being encouraged to settle and finish their disagreements and to work together for the best interests of each other and the children, the system pits them against each other and often sets them on a course of spite and revenge. It is hardly surprising that the results of a divorce or separation can be battered self-esteem and a lack of self-confidence in both partners and the children involved. Often the problems a new family experiences are left over from the old relationship.

Children become the prime targets for much of the anger and grief simply because of their position in the middle. If the adults refuse to listen to each other, they both know they will receive a hearing from the children and probably hope that any complaint will be passed on. Sometimes the adults simply do not realize how their feelings are being expressed and how they are affecting their sons and daughters. At other times, however, the children are quite deliberately used as a means of punishing the ex-partner. The adult with whom the children live may make access difficult, by not having children ready when the other parent comes to collect them or even by 'forgetting' an arrangement and sending them out to do something else. The estranged parent, in turn, may arrive late, not come at all or keep the children beyond the agreed time. The ones who suffer most in such situations are the children themselves. It is notable that studies suggest that children whose parents have divorced are likely to have lower expectations and less self-confidence than children from happy families. They are more likely to be under-achievers, to smoke, drink and have a lower income when adults.

One of the problems experienced in a family after a divorce or separation, and particularly in a blended family, is that the existence of the other parent prevents the remaining or new family from becoming a cohesive unit. Many parents struggling to cope with children feel that if there were no contact with the estranged partner, everything else would be much easier. Ann, who lives with her new partner,

Sean, and her two daughters aged nine and eleven, wishes desperately that the children did not see her husband. After two years of living apart from him she has asked for a divorce, but he is contesting this and will not agree to a divorce by mutual consent. She may have to wait for five years before she can divorce him on the grounds of having lived apart for that time.

> I would really like to stop him having anything to do with us. Each time the kids see him there's trouble. They get wound up about it beforehand and they are always in a real state afterwards. Sean could be a perfectly good father to them. He likes my kids and it really could be good. Most of the time they like him too, but whenever they've been with their dad they come back and for days afterwards it's absolute hell. They're rude to Sean, cheeky to me and we have arguments. They won't eat and they don't even sleep properly. At the moment he sees them once a month, but he wants to see them once a week. Can you imagine what it would be like if I had to cope with this every week?

The main reason for the problems in blended families is that what the adults want or need is not the same and indeed is often at odds with what the children want or need. Adults may need complete separation, though it must be said that to try to forget or deny that a former partner was a part of your life is to deny a part of yourself, which is hardly healthy. But for children it is never helpful to deny contact with or the recognition of the role of the other parent.

In many cases there will be some or even a considerable amount of time between the ending of the original relationship and the formation of the new family. This may also be so when a partnership is dissolved and a new one made almost immediately if the actual presence within the family of the old partner has been minimal. The dynamic between parent and child in the time between the loss of the old family and the acquisition of the new may have a considerable effect on how everyone in the blended family gets on.

If the parent has leaned heavily on the child for emotional support or practical help, the child may find it hard to hand their new adult place in the family over to a new partner. Children may be under pressure from everyone else to be happy at belonging once again to what society considers to be a proper family, but feel that their positions inside this new family are more of a loss than a gain. Children used to being relied on or respected as equal members may suddenly find themselves thrust back into dependency or into the background. Linda's son Pat has not welcomed the intrusion into their lives of her new partner. Linda divorced her first husband six years ago when Pat was ten. Four years later she met Eric, and he moved in with them just over a year ago. Pat

> was very jealous, and the two of them were like two roosters in a farmyard. I should have thought of it, but it never occurred to me at the time. But of course Pat had been the man of the house for going on five years. I suppose I depended on him too much and he'd grown used to it. I thought it would be a relief for him not to have to worry about me, because he used to do that. He used to stay at home instead of going out with his friends sometimes so I wouldn't be alone. It's not surprising, then, that when Eric came along Pat felt he'd been pushed out.

Two dynamics are present in any family: the relationship of the adults to each other, and of the children and adults.

One of the big differences with a stepfamily is that children predate the couple rather than the other way round, so that the couple establish themselves alongside the children. Adults who once considered themselves to be primarily parents may now see themselves primarily as newly-weds – roles that do not sit easily together and may conflict. Furthermore, rather than having some degree of choice as to whether or not you fill your lives and your home with children, you may feel this becomes something beyond your control.

When Carol and Philip started living together, she knew that his four children played an important part in his life. At first they lived with their mother, but one day, with no warning at all, one of them turned up after having had a disagreement with her, and moved in; he stayed for thirteen years.

> Overnight we were not just a couple with minor responsibilities, seeing children only at the weekends or in school holidays. It became a much more regular thing. Gradually, two more of the family came to live with us, even if it was just for university vacations or for a few months. We've had three out of four actually through the door.

Trying to build a new relationship when one or both partners have children is anything but easy. Quite apart from the emotional issues, there are the boring practical problems, such as having to get a babysitter or finding time to be alone with the children in the house. Which social events do you want to share with your children? If you go on holiday together, is it with or without the youngsters?

Jean remembers trying to combine a romantic social life with motherhood.

It was quite difficult having to go back to dating all over again. I'd been a settled married lady for ten years and it felt very strange to be dating again with all those 'Will he, won't he? Do I, don't I?' sort of worries. It was like having to remember dance steps you've forgotten. To be honest, the worst part was the way my two carried on. It was like having your parents standing over you making horrible remarks about your clothing or your new boyfriend, but ten times worse. They took the mickey something rotten, and I really did feel there was a bit of an edge in it.

Sometimes that edge can be expressed in stronger terms, as Kate found when an old boyfriend, George, took her home to meet his family.

George was obviously nervous when he introduced me to his two daughters. But that was nothing to the way I felt. I can remember it to this day because they seemed strangely calculating for such young children, or at least that's what I thought. It had never occurred to me to remember how very definite you can feel at that age. Anyway, I thought I was making a good impression until Kerry, the eldest, caught me alone in the living-room. She then proceeded to calmly tell me that neither they nor their dad needed anyone else and I shouldn't think I could waltz in and take over. They'd seen off quite a few of his girlfriends and would do the same to me. I was totally gobsmacked, didn't know what to say and simply gaped at her. I spent hours debating whether to tell George, but I decided in the end, just as I'm sure she'd known, that there wasn't much point, he wouldn't believe it. I honestly tried, but it was soon very clear that she meant what she said. I finished the relationship and I've since married someone else. That was ten years ago and I sometimes think about him and his children. We have a mutual friend and I know from her that he's never remarried. I'm sure the situation suited those kids while they were growing up, but I wonder what they think of it now. It must be rather sad when you want to go out and have your own family to know that you've kept your dad from having a helpmate in his life.

The problems of establishing a new relationship in the shadow of children are often such that it is tempting to keep the children right out of it. Some blended families seem to start 'in spite of the children', almost by ignoring that the children exist. When Alex first met Jan, he was not aware she had two children from an earlier marriage.

Jan didn't tell me that she had children until we'd been seeing each other for over a year. She said that she hadn't kept it from me deliberately, it was just that she had always arranged it that we'd see each other while the kids were with their father, and she was always keener to see me at my place or out than to take me back to her place. Once I got over the shock, I was quite happy about the idea of our going on together, and I was even happier at the idea of our getting together for good. But I must admit I'd sort of pushed the idea of the kids into the back of my mind and that was where they stayed. I didn't meet them properly until the weekend after we decided to get married and I never really thought about how they were going to affect the marriage at all. As you can imagine, it was one hell of a shock when it finally came home to me that I wasn't just marrying Jan but taking on her kids as well.

Even if new partners are more than aware that they are not getting just a partner but taking on the package deal of adult plus children, it may still be hard to experience what life is going to be like until quite late on in the proceedings. This is particularly true if it is going to be a 'weekend parent' arrangement and the children live elsewhere, or if the children are going to split their time equally between households. During courtship the children's presence may not have been felt because they were with their other parent while the new couple were together.

Whether or not the children have got to know the new partner well, and whether or not they have been able to build up their own relationship with the new partner, finally breaking the news that marriage or living together is planned is bound to be difficult. Philip made a point of telling his four children when he and Carol, who is some twenty years younger than he is, decided that they were going to live together.

> When the relationship started to get serious, I actually had all the children round for the weekend without Carol and explained that we weren't going to get married in the near future but that Carol was going to move in. I sat them around the meal table and said, 'This is the situation. Like it or lump it.' They just sat there and looked at me, and one of them called me a dirty old man. They all came up the next weekend. They didn't usually all come up at the same time because they had their own lives.

As Carol remembers:

> We did seem to have a particularly good turnout the weekend that we were officially living together. They all came to have a look. Then there was a sort of

council of war in the spare room, all of the children discussing this very important topic: 'Do you think they'll sleep together?' 'No.' And 'If they get married, will she be our stepmother?' 'God, I hope not.' But you might as well have this response as not. I wouldn't have liked party manners at the time and then finding out two years later that they hated me. In retrospect, the whole thing seems funny, but I found it quite stressful at the time.

Christine met her husband Gregory seven years ago, and they have been married for three years. They too found they were nervous about breaking the news to his three children from a previous marriage and spending their first weekend all together.

The worst thing about our getting together was telling the kids. It was a complete non-event. They just sort of said 'Well, yeah.' That was worse in preparation. I'll never forget the first weekend they came and stayed – this was before Gregory and I were living together – and explaining to them where we were all going to sleep and trying not to seem anxious or worried about it. The older two smirked, and the four-year-old said, 'No, Dad, don't sleep with Christine, you come and sleep with me.' That was awful, wondering what we were doing to this little girl's world because suddenly Daddy was going to sleep with this strange woman. I remember now being quite scared about that because they are inevitably excluded from our intimate relationship. When you are a parent, that doesn't even cross your mind.

One of the reasons for the tensions that may surround this announcement is that children will always harbour the hope that their parents will get back together again, however unreasonable or even undesirable this may be. The announcement that the new person is not just a passing fancy temporarily taking the place of the estranged parent but a permanent partner can cause enormous anger and pain. Marrying or moving in with a new partner can be seen by children as the final statement that the relationship between their parents is over for good, and it may be strenuously resisted. The fact that the new adult may be tolerated or even liked by the children will not necessarily make any difference. Deirdre and Paul, for instance, got on well and it was clear that he had no wish to have her eliminated from the equation. But that did not stop him from hoping that his parents might be reunited.

He obviously hated having parents living apart. Several times he'd say he wished we all lived together – Laura, himself, James and me.

Grandparents and in-laws may, deliberately or unwittingly, be at the heart of some of your problems. They may find it hard to pitch their responses towards a new partner. Is the new adult, are the new children, trespassers and interlopers, or are they welcome additions? This may be more of a factor if grandparents have taken a parental role at some point before or while the new relationship was being established, and feel their place in the children's lives is being taken by the new adult. Or there may be friction if they feel the new adult or the children exert a claim that is somehow fraudulent. Deirdre has found her mother's attitude towards Paul, her partner's son, particularly painful.

My mother doesn't accept the relationship at all. She made it clear that she intends leaving her money to a trust fund with the interest going to me in my lifetime, but the capital to the trust. The point of that is to make absolutely sure that Paul, not being my real child, will not inherit her money, or possessions that are part of our family inheritance. I think that's awful, because I feel he is my family and I want him to have things that have a meaning to me, such as paintings that belonged to my grandmother. They have only met once, when she was polite and charming. But she never suggested another meeting and when I talk about him, she makes no comment. When I told her recently that he had got a good degree, she said James must be pleased, but no more. She doesn't consider him my son, so she certainly doesn't see herself as even a quasi-grandmother. He is a stranger to her and nothing to do with her, she feels. My feelings about him have nothing to do with it. If I was married to James, she might feel differently. But without a legal tie, she sees no emotional tie.

There may be a good deal more to face than a relative's refusal to become involved or to recognize a relationship. In many families the attitudes and feelings of grandparents and other relatives are shown more forcefully. Marvin, who is twenty-one, finds some of his family are positively hostile towards his father. His parents split up when he was eleven and his father moved in with a girlfriend he has since married.

On my mum's side of the family there was strong resentment against my dad. If my grandmother met him, I don't think she'd talk to him. That opinion is shared by most of Mum's family.

Often relatives or friends offer what is considered to be support without anyone bothering to check whether it is welcomed by the people meant to be helped. Paul has learned that

> it's very easy for even the most well meaning of relatives to 'take sides', when what you really want is cheering up. If your father or mother is beyond redemption, then fair enough. If not, it's better for others to say nothing if they can't be constructive. Relatives' loyalty is to their side of the family rather than the success of the relationship. More importantly, if one part of a stepfamily feels that other avenues of help are cut off due to this sort of attitude, then any problems will multiply.

Sometimes the failure to check has the opposite effect. Those on the fringes may do nothing harmful but nothing constructive either, because they have not thought it necessary to lend a hand. Carol, who took on Philip's four children, did not receive much help from relatives or friends.

> It wasn't because they were ill disposed. It was because we looked as if we were managing reasonably well. Philip's family were unreservedly welcoming to me. They were positive and very complimentary. There was no disapproval, which was a big help. You can imagine how I would have felt if not only had I had a little bit of hostility from the children but also a wall put up by members of the family who for some reason wanted to protect him from me.

It is quite common for responses to be varied. Each child in the same family may react differently. You may find not only that the original family is divided, with parents at loggerheads and the children in between, and stepchildren and step-parent at odds, but that children within the blended family disagree. Marvin says that when his father left, his sister, who is three years his junior,

> was affected badly and she has a real attitude about our father now. The only way he can make up for the fact that he walked out on us is to give her lots of money and buy her things. Often, she can't be bothered to go and see him at all.

Becoming a new stepfather or stepmother can mean many changes, for example of status. The adult is no longer a single person or a widow or a widower but a partner or spouse and, perhaps, a parent. Carol found the transition from living on her own to living with Philip and having his four children visit as often as they liked quite a shock.

> It was lovely, but overwhelming in terms of the practical side of things – I bought this house on my own, single woman, single lifestyle, and suddenly I had a family and all their stuff. That was really overwhelming, the lack of both physical and emotional space.

The lack of outside recognition of these very changes may be another difficulty, as Christine found. Her partner Gregory's three children visited once a fortnight and were a permanent part of his life.

> I was working when I first became a stepmother with three children. I saw myself as that even though they weren't with us all the time. They had to have my consideration, my thought, whatever, and there was no forum to do that. I remember thinking that when people have babies they take photos into the office and everyone gives cards and congratulations and the event is very much acknowledged. People see that this person's life is changing because of the baby. Even

when you adopt, there's all sorts of showering of gifts. There was nothing for me. I walked into the office one day and we'd had all three children for the weekend. People knew, but there was no way of making it an event. I suppose that if we had married, there would have been, 'Oh, you've taken on a husband who has a family.' But we didn't feel that was wise at the time.

You may have to consider purely practical issues. A new family may mean a move to a new house, a new part of town or even an entirely unfamiliar location. Children may then have to contend with finding their way not only through a new set-up at home but round a new neighbourhood, a new school and new friends, as well as coping with the attendant loss of the old ones. Practical difficulties may also occur in managing two homes for the children. Essential equipment for school may be at one location while the children are at another and parents may find it hard to know what is going on. Matthew, for instance, lives with his father and his second wife, Marian, and keeping up to date with his mother is sometimes less than straightforward.

I have to keep phoning Mum and telling her what's happening. It's a bit awkward. You tend to forget that one parent knows and the other doesn't.

Paul's parents were divorced when he was very young. Paul lived with his mother but kept in contact with his father, James, though this has not always gone smoothly.

The worst thing was going through a patch from about sixteen to twenty-two when I didn't communicate as much as I would have liked to have done with my father. And, of course, when either of us made 'an effort', then it just felt worse. It's quite easy when you live apart to forget that you have in effect a 'separate' life that often makes this effort vital to maintain a pleasant normality, and I think that perhaps my father didn't/doesn't think about this as much as he could. This is partly due to his lifestyle, but then again I'm like that too.

Being part of two different lifestyles can cause confusion for young people. Jack, who is seventeen, is an only child, and his parents separated when he was seven. His father is now married to a woman in her late thirties and Jack stays with his mother and her 66-year-old partner of the last ten years. Both Jack's parents are in their fifties.

It's extremely strange to compare the two families. My dad and his wife are extremely happy together and have an enormous social life. My mum and stepdad, on the other hand, seem to have about one friend that they go out with every two months or so, which is a bit ridiculous. I think this is because my dad has married someone a lot younger, and my mum's married some-one a lot older. My dad gets to sort of relive part of his life that he might have missed, while my mum just skips out half of hers and becomes sort of retired with nothing to do.

Continuity and consistency are important to children and can be hard enough to sustain within a family when parents who live together have different styles or approaches to bringing up children. Where parents live apart and other adults are involved, the likelihood of divergence increases. This may result in the stepchild resenting the position held by the new step-parent. Sometimes the statement 'You can't tell me what to do because you aren't my *real* mother/father' is a heartfelt howl of protest at the displacement.

Loyalty to and love for the missing parent makes it very difficult for the child to offer anything but hostility towards the new adult in his or her life. But sometimes bolshie behaviour is a genuine reaction to demands that are simply not understood. Each family has its own routines, expectations, rules and beliefs. Christine and Gregory, whose three children stay once a fortnight, find this can lead to conflict.

> There are some ways in which it would be easier. One factor is that their mum's value system is different to ours and so we all have this awful adjustment to make every fortnight. There are certain rules or things that we feel are important and that they know they have to get back into. If they were here all the time it would perhaps become second nature that they did things like make their beds.

Where a blended family sets up home can be terribly important. Whether the parent and children move in with the new partner, the new partner joins the family home or they all move in to new living accommodation can affect what ensues. A step-parent moving in may be resented by the children, who will see the newcomer as an invader. A family moving in with a new partner may not feel truly at home and the children particularly could be uneasy and alienated in their new surroundings. A totally fresh start would seem to be the ideal compromise, yet children may need the comfort of familiarity and dislike being uprooted.

The space a blended family has and how it is allocated will have considerable bearing on what is happening at a time when relationships are still being defined and are still fragile. If money is scarce, or a family is trying to fit into a space not intended for that number of people, children who previously had their own rooms may have to share. This can lead to a great deal of bitterness, especially if two sets of children are being blended who resent forced proximity to step-siblings. If the privacy and security of your own room represent a haven at a time when the privacy and security of what you had thought was your family is being burst asunder, losing this can cause anxiety. The space available for children who visit at weekends or for holidays can play a part in determining whether or not relationships go well. Deirdre, who has lived with James for eighteen years, remembers with regret the way they handled contact with his son when he was younger.

We made a stupid mistake when we bought our first place together. It was a one-bedroomed flat near the city centre. If we had had any sense, we would have got two bedrooms, but James thought it was silly spending money we couldn't afford, or having to live further out than we wanted, for the sake of having a room for Paul's occasional visits. Big mistake. He may not have stayed a lot, but when he did, it just rubbed it in that he didn't have a place in our lives but slept in a put-up bed. He didn't have a stake in our lives, so it seemed. Every time he came, he'd walk around checking up that everything he remembered was still there. And because the place was small, we would always be going out – on treats. That wasn't right. What he wanted, and we really needed, was just to slop around and be together as a family. We would go out and he would get tired and bored and frustrated. And we would feel panicky that money was short, and get annoyed that he wasn't grateful for the treats. We would bicker, that would terrify him and things would get fraught. In our new house, we have two spare rooms and we've given him a key. As far as I'm concerned, he has a room here and can come and go as he pleases. Of course it's a bit bloody late, and I wish we'd done this fifteen years ago.

Cramming into a small space may affect your ability to be like a 'normal' family, especially if this crush only happens on some occasions, such as weekends when the children come to stay. Christine admits:

> One of the difficulties has been a small house that has sometimes made it a choice of having all the children and no friends because we can't accommodate them all together. This makes me sad because our friends don't get to spend time with my stepchildren as well as our own children.

Holidays, festivals and anniversaries such as Christmas, Easter and birthdays may assume frightening proportions in a blended family. The wider family often puts pressure on parents and children at such times, and this can be further complicated if you are part of a blended family, as Sarah and her second husband, Jeff, have found. They have two daughters of their own and a son by her first husband, Robin.

> Christmas used to be difficult enough when Robin and my parents both used to compete with each other and try to put pressure on us to spend Christmas with them. But now I've got both of them wanting to see the grandchildren and Jeff's parents joining in too.

Family traditions can also become battlefields. Instead of being a time of celebration, Fiona now finds that Christmas is the cue for terrible arguments in her family. She had two children by her first husband when she married Dave, who also had two children by his former wife, Sally. Fiona and Dave have since had two children of their own.

> It was always a tradition in my family that we would open a small present on Christmas Eve and then open

our stockings all together before breakfast on Christmas morning. Then we'd have presents from the family when they all came for Christmas lunch and finally special, large presents around the tree after tea. Well, Dave has been used to a gigantic present-opening session in the morning, and it's what his kids expect. My children kick up an almighty fuss and really hate it if it's not done our way, and his do exactly the same if it's not done their way. It all seems totally out of proportion, but we can't find a way round it.

What is being fought over is not the event itself but what it means. And what it means, of course, is security and continuity. Finding a compromise that will be accepted can stretch your ingenuity and you may even be tempted to abandon the whole thing in despair. Carol married Philip nine years ago and found juggling Christmas arrangements with his ex-wife and four children prompted them to do just that.

We even gave up one Christmas and scandalized everyone by going away. We got fed up waiting for the two hours when we could expect to see the children on some unimportant occasion between Christmas and the New Year. Philip said, 'Blow this for a lark. We've both worked hard this year, let's go away.' It was quite spontaneous. Mind you, we paid for it. His son arrived on the doorstep when we got back and stayed for thirteen years.

You can create problems for yourselves by going to extremes, by insisting either that the new family conforms exactly to the routines and traditions that you or they have known before or that, symbolic of the change, everything must be different.

Money is often given as the main cause of conflict in second marriages. It is easy to see why this is so. A divorced wife can claim an increase in maintenance for her children if her ex-husband's situation changes. If he remarries, and his second wife works, her income and her assets will be taken into account. He is not ordered to pay more simply because his new wife is well off. The assumption is that if her income contributes to maintaining his new family, more of his money can be released for his first family. Similarly, if his first wife remarries into affluence, his responsibilities may continue because the law sees him as paying for the maintenance of his children, not her. It is worth noting, in these days of equality, that both parents are considered to be responsible for their children. If the mother has left and the father is caring for their children, she may be the one who is expected to contribute. Stepfamilies are often more economically disadvantaged than comparable natural families. This may be because the men involved are also paying for their first family and many stepmothers do not work. (The reasons for their not doing so will be discussed in the next chapter.)

Money becomes a focus for disagreement because it is a symbol. It is a convenient means by which an abandoned spouse can continue to vent his or her anger, pain and bitterness upon a partner after a marriage has broken down. And it may be used as a means of sustaining the often fragile connection between a parent and their children. James did not see Paul on a regular basis, but there were frequent visits. On some of these Paul's mother would make requests that sparked resentment in James and his partner, Deirdre.

Laura, to give her credit, was amazing. Whenever we did see her, she would play what we called the territorial Game – 'I was here first.' She'd talk about old mutual friends or tell stories of their past. But it was never malicious – never against me. It was an understandable attempt to affirm the fact that she had been there first. It did upset me a bit then, but now I can accept it. What did upset me desperately was the way she would send Paul for a weekend with a list of clothes to buy. We were broke and she had a pretty comfortable family. We would get the clothes, with Paul choosing what he wanted, and he'd never wear them again. Yes, yes, now I understand the pressures on him and on her. Money is such a symbol, and it was important for both of them to see James proving he still cared. But I'd get furious and I suppose it wasn't really the money itself but the feeling it was taking something away from us. Stupid really, but very real at the time.

Tragically, this attempt to remind everyone concerned that the estranged parent still is or should be responsible and involved often goes wrong. By two years after the divorce, 50 per cent of men have ceased having any contact with the family they left.

Generosity, genuine or apparent, on the part of the non-resident partner can be just as much a weapon as meanness can. Valerie's ex-husband Tom has recently reappeared, having had no contact with his children for nearly eight years. He has taken out the two eldest, Lucy and Mike, and lavished gifts on them, but ignores his younger son, seven-year-old Thomas. Tom will buy Mike and Lucy expensive treats for which they are far too young, such as champagne, but he contributes just £26 a month for the three children and has done that only for the last few years.

Tom uses money. I've been struggling for years to

make do on what little we have and he's always been totally haphazard with maintenance. When he's got them for the weekend, he'll flash money around and buy them treats, making a big deal about it so they feel like kings. Then they come back to me bitching about my meanness and going on about how wonderful and generous he is.

Money can also be used by members of a wider family network to underline perceptions of who does and does not belong inside the family proper. Relatives may give presents of unequal value or may not give any at all, almost as a way of saying that a particular child does not exist in their eyes. Fiona, who already had two children when she married Dave, found present-giving was being used to make a point.

Dave had a major split with his mother for many years over the way she treated our children. From the beginning, she made a big point of giving my two presents on their birthdays and at Christmas and made the most unholy fuss about it if they weren't properly grateful. Here was she welcoming them into her family as her grandchildren! But what was really and nastily obvious was the fact that the presents she gave them and me were totally inferior to the presents she gave Sally, Dave's ex-wife, and her children. Then when Dave and I had two children of our own, they got different presents than my two as well, because, after all, they were her 'proper' grandchildren.

Similarly, children may reject gifts given by step-relations as a way of rejecting overtures. Sheila has been married to Marty for a year and a half. She has three children – boys aged sixteen and six and a girl of nine – from her first marriage and Marty has boys of fifteen and twelve. Michael, the elder,

has remained at boarding-school even though his younger brother has asked to stay home with us. We know he is unhappy, so my mother wanted to make a gesture and sent him the sort of things she can remember liking when she was away at school – a tuck-box and some books and magazines. She didn't hear a word from him and I think was genuinely worried that they had gone astray. He rings Marty sometimes, so we were able to check that he had received them. But even when we asked him to write and say thanks, he didn't. So now she just washes her hands of him.

Weekend or holiday step-parenting can be far more difficult than full-time. The children may be seen less, but there is often little control over when, where and how. Deirdre had mixed feelings about Paul's visits.

Laura used to ring up and say, 'Paul really needs to see his father and would like to come for the weekend.' It may have been totally inconvenient for us and mean we had to cancel plans we had, but we really had no choice. Then he would arrive and be in a really foul mood, sulking all weekend. We would then be fed up that we'd had our weekend spoiled on his insistence and he hadn't enjoyed it. It took us an awful long time to realize that what was going on was that Laura had needed a break, possibly because she had a boyfriend she wanted to spend a romantic weekend with, and it was her choice, not Paul's, that he come down. He, of course, had had his own plans for seeing friends or just mucking around at home, and that had been totally thrown out of kilter. It wasn't her fault, because I can see the difficulties she was living with, but it really was hell on wheels for all of us.

Control can be an issue in other ways with part-time parenting, as Gregory and his wife, Christine, found out. His three children visit every fortnight. In Christine's experience,

> there is a common view that because we have the kids part time we are somehow luckier and get a break. There are quite definitely some factors, which make it much more difficult. For example, Gregory pays maintenance for them, but we have no control over what clothes, equipment or things are bought, and we have them to pay for on top of expenses for their weekends. The biggest thing is that when they come to us, it isn't their home. Also the two eldest are now teenagers and I think at that age they don't want to spend a whole weekend with their dad and another adult. They actually have a healthy lifestyle that often excludes parents and can't follow them here. They haven't got their things here, and most of all they haven't got their friends here. We have this divided life where we try and keep in touch as much as we can, and then here they are. We are then their total entertainment and that is very difficult.

This toing and froing between families and homes is probably the worst aspect for everyone in a new extended family – the children, the full-time and the part-time parent and the step-parent. If the parent who has left ceases to have any sort of contact with or access to their children, however, it does not make the situation any easier. We will discuss this area more fully in Chapter 5.

The Children Act recognizes the enormous importance of the biological parent to children, one aspect of which is retaining the name of the birth father, even if the mother has remarried and changed her name and he is no longer a part of their lives. This can make it easier for the young people concerned to keep a sense of their own identity. Disagreements over what children should call their step-parents and how they should refer to each other underline the fact that there are no guidelines to help us consider and define the role of step-parents. Deirdre finds it difficult to describe her relationship to Paul.

James and I have been together for eighteen years and we've a permanent, stable partnership. But we've never actually married, so Paul isn't my stepson, not offi-cially, and I'm not his stepmother. I have a feeling that the fact that he didn't call either of his parents Mum and Dad all the time did help. He calls them and refers to them by their own first names. In fact, he never really calls James Dad – unless he's taking the mickey and calling him Pater. So it seemed less of a glaring addition to have 'Deirdre' added to Laura and James. Mind you, we had some awkward moments. He once introduced me to his headmaster as 'my father's friend', and to a schoolfriend's mother as James's 'flatmate'. I do sometimes call him my stepson, because it's so complicated to have to go through the rigmarole. But I have sometimes felt awkward, as if I might be claiming a relationship with him that he might not want to acknowledge. I think he's always been happy with it. He calls me Deirdre sometimes, but more often it's Dree, which has become his own special pet name for me.

Certainly many step-parents find particular conflicts arise if they try to insist that stepchildren call them by any title the child is not happy to acknowledge.

The fact that the people in blended families have no blood relationship can lead to deeper, darker and more troubling difficulties than those already discussed. Studies show that stepfathers are five times more likely to sexually abuse children than birth fathers. The reasons for this may be many, varied and complex, but one element could be that because the child is not their own, one further taboo against doing it is simply removed. Other men or boys in the family may also find it possible to sexually abuse a child that much more easily if the child is under their nominal authority; while they may be considered to be a brother, an uncle or a grandfather, deep down they may feel themselves to have no connection to the child.

A sexual relationship between stepchildren may be problematical in that to everyone else it is taboo because the two are viewed as being related. Sharron's father and Richard's mother married when the children were both thirteen.

I wasn't too keen on my stepfather at first, but I liked Sharron from the beginning. We were really close for the first couple of years and then our feelings got even deeper and closer. Our parents never said anything. I think that was because they hoped it would all go away. My best friend knew that Sharron was special to me, 'cos he fancied her too and we used to joke that he had no chance when it was her brother she liked best. Things turned a bit sour and came to a head when this old bat living next door saw us kissing and started spreading rumours. I think people had forgotten by then that Mum and Dad had really only been married for four years.

Eventually this social worker turned up and put the fear of God into us, and it wasn't until she'd gone on at us for what must have been more than an hour that my mum suddenly said that Sharron and I were not even related. We are both going to university next year – the same one – and the good part is that because our surnames are different, because I never changed mine even though my mother did, no one need know. I hope we stay together and I can't see our feelings for each other changing. Maybe after three years away it will be different, but I have a feeling that the only way we are not going to live with tongues wagging and fingers pointing at us is to move away.

Heightened awareness of the lack of boundaries between adults and children in a stepfamily can lead to other forms of difficulty. Parents may find it hard to talk to their children about sexual matters, even about the most basic sex education, for fear of somehow stepping over an invisible and shifting line. The very fact that one or both parents may be openly conducting a sexual relationship at a time in their lives when sex might otherwise have faded into the background can have an undesirable effect. Teenage children, particularly girls, may become involved prematurely in a sexual relationship of their own. Alternatively, they may find the idea of dating and showing an interest in the opposite sex frightening and disgusting.

You are always undeniably responsible for children to whom you have given birth, and you have to accept that. When you take on a child after his or her birth, you may be constantly reminded that you could send them away or walk away yourself, that you have a choice and can say no. This may create a frame of mind that allows dissatisfaction or criticism, or allows you to conceive of an alternative, which may be at the core, or explain the particular intensity, of many of the problems encountered by step-parents. Normal, natural families do not, we often believe, have all these difficulties, and if only these children were our own, everything would be different. Any trouble that arises is often blamed on our being in a blended family. If we are to understand whether this is fair and what we can do about it, we need to explore why the problems outlined here occur. To do this we will examine first the adults' and then the children's point of view.

4

The Adult's View

When you become part of a blended family, you cannot help but go into it with views about yourself, about the other people involved and the situation itself. We have already looked at how the myths and conventions our society has about step-relationships may condition what we see and experience. You are likely, however, to enter a step-relationship with private emotions and possibly unrealistically high expectations that have been shaped by your own personal experience. The ending of a previous relationship may have left you struggling with a sense of failure. In addition to being perfect, a new relationship may be required to cure all the hurt and conquer any doubts about your worth and attractiveness. But the presence of other people – children and ex-spouses – who seem to claim as much love and attention as you do may give rise to jealousy and insecurity. All of this will affect how you and your partner form your new blended family.

Everyone else is going to find themselves reacting to your set of responses, whether you or they are aware of what you are doing. And everybody concerned is going to have their own set of responses and you are going to be reacting to these too. None of this is anybody's fault and no one is to blame for how he or she is feeling or behaving. But if you can understand what you are feeling and why, you may be a long way towards dealing with the specific problems, explaining yourself to others and perhaps making adjustments yourself or helping others to do so too. It is also of enormous benefit if you can understand what the young people are experiencing, and we will be dealing with that in the next chapter.

It cannot be stressed too strongly or too often that all blended families necessarily begin in the aftermath of a tragedy or a failed relationship. You may think that you are beginning, or desperately want to begin, with a totally clean sheet, but this simply is not possible. The problem with suppressing feelings, hiding them either from others or from yourself, is that they have the nasty habit of emerging in often unexpected ways, as Heather found.

I went to see a counsellor after I'd been married for two years because we were quarrelling a lot and I used to get crying fits. I said that the main reason I'd get upset, which I couldn't tell my new husband, was that I kept seeing my ex-husband around town and I felt very bad about leaving him. I was now beginning to wonder whether I had done the right thing because he looked so sad, or so I thought. The counsellor suggested that perhaps *I* was the one who was most upset about the break-up and that I hadn't sorted it out in my own mind. She pointed out that in fact, from what I said, it was clear that he had made a new life and was perfectly happy to get on with it. I got really angry with her, but after a few weeks of going and chatting with her I realized she was quite right. In the end I decided I hadn't made a mistake when I ended it with him and I'm far happier now in my new marriage. But I think if I hadn't been able to face up to my very mixed feelings, I would never have been able to put it behind me and move on.

It is quite common to sense an emotional link to someone

even though you are planning to divorce them or have already done so, and even after you have met, fallen in love with and married someone new. Relationships end by a complicated process and not simply because one partner falls in love with someone else, or realizes they no longer love the other partner. If you are going to understand how 'leftover' feelings from an earlier relationship may affect a new one, you need to understand how relationships tend to come apart.

While relationships break up in their own individual ways, the steps to a breakdown are often broadly similar. There is definitely a general pattern to the process by which couples who were once one unit come apart.

When a marriage begins to disintegrate, one or both partners may realize they are not happy. They may try to hide this, pretend worries do not exist or hope that by ignoring them they will go away. Frequently one of the partners will begin a new interest at this point. It could start as a way of filling time, but then become a means to develop an identity that is not simply dependent on the relationship.

At this stage any thought of separation is still probably a long way off and the other partner may be invited to join in the new interest. But if this offer is rejected, and particularly if the interest makes the person feel better than they do in the relationship, then a form of separation has already taken place and the two people have begun to live in separate worlds. Open rows, public complaints and more time spent away from the partnership may follow. If this has no effect and the other partner remains unaware that anything is wrong, the first may find another person outside the relationship to talk to and confide in.

This third party could be a member of the clergy, a child, an old school friend, a divorce lawyer – or a lover. But whoever it is, by this time the partnership is at an end. One of you will be ready to leave, though the other may want the relationship to continue. The person leaving may already have recognized and even fully mourned the death of the relationship, while the other partner is still totally committed to it and will then behave like someone who has lost a partner in a fatal car crash. Most of us have seen (or experienced) situations in which one partner is off building a new life at the same time as the other has not even begun to feel separate and is bombarding friends with endless repetitions of 'What happened? We were so close, we told each other everything and did everything together.'

Some people never truly recognize or admit that a relationship is over and they may remain 'psychologically married' for ever, even if they are legally divorced, have entered into new relationships or have remarried. If the separation is not mutual and total, there will always be a degree of this emotional hangover. There is no formal 'funeral' at the end of a relationship – no body, no coffin and therefore, in many cases, no admission of a death at all. Since we are taught in this society that it is important to be a couple, we usually enter into relationships expecting them to last, and it is obviously hard to let go without a struggle. Women often take longer to separate than men, as they can be nervous of being on their own. And, curiously, either sex can experience all these difficulties even if they are the ones choosing to leave the relationship. Just because you were the person who left or opted for divorce does not mean that you were the one who emotionally separated.

It is absolutely essential to sort out how you feel about the relationship that has failed, whether it is your own or your partner's, before you can happily make and sustain a new one. It is very human to look at a failed relationship and want to wipe it completely from the record. To say, in effect, 'This was a mistake and I want to totally forget that I ever loved/that my partner ever loved this person.' This is hard enough when you are an individual, because doing this successfully means removing a part of yourself. You are, after all, the sum of everything in your past. But it presents particular difficulties and is even more important when there are children from the relationship. Saying you do not love the former partner and never have implies that you do not love or want a part of the children either. Whether you demand this of yourself or of your new partner, the likelihood is that it will cause conflict and pain for all of you. In such a charged atmosphere both step-parent and birth parent may feel threatened if they see habits or behaviour in the children that they think come from the absent parent. If there is anything you do not like in the child it may be tempting to say, 'The child doesn't get that from you, and certainly not from me, so it must be from him/her.'

Often the strong insistence that children from an old relationship can be parented so much better by the new partner is a way of trying to rewrite history. You are trying to convince yourself that the former partner was a mistake, but the children are not part of the same mistake because they really belong to the new partner. The two adults in the new relationship may then pull in very different directions: the one who is bringing children with them will be encouraging the new partner to take over the role and position of the missing parent; the one who is taking on someone else's children may not want even to acknowledge these children exist because they are a reminder of a past love.

But what of the situation where one adult has children who live for most of the time with the ex-partner? A 'weekend parent' may be zealously trying to retain a link from the past while progressively being frozen out by whoever has the children permanently. On the other hand, he or she may be involved in severing those links, pretending children or an ex-partner are no longer important, causing pain and confusion in the discarded family, who make increasingly desperate attempts to keep in touch. Children may be deliberately kept out of the new partnership as much as possible, often as a means of punishing the ex-partner, with the excuse that it prevents their unhappiness. This is likely to punish the children instead and to warp their attitudes to the step-relationship.

All these unhappy feelings clearly have to come to earth somewhere. Everyone has a justified reason for feeling bitter and angry at someone else in the pattern. Whether you are male or female, the full-time or the weekend parent or the new partner of either, you will naturally have strong emotions about everyone else involved. In some situations one person may be an easy target. When Deirdre and James started living together, she had to come to terms with the fact that he had a seven-year-old son from his marriage.

> I think I always loved Paul as a person, but resented him for being a complication, if you can see what I mean. The person and the complication were two totally separate things. The complication, of course, was the fact that it meant we had a tie both to him and to his mother. I would have liked James and me to have been two entirely free individuals. I suppose that's unreasonable, because you never are entirely free from family. But it was as if something kept dragging up the past and there was nothing we could do about it. For many years there were really only two things that could cause an argument between the two of us – my mother and his son.

A new partner implicated in the break-up of a relationship or marriage will almost certainly become a scapegoat to the abandoned parent, his or her children and the relatives, often of both families. But the desire to blame someone and to direct the concern and confusion in the aftermath of a disintegrated relationship may mean that a new partner who had nothing to do with the breakdown is still blamed. Philip says of his first wife and divorce:

> I met Carol a long time after we had separated, but if you talk to Joe Bloggs today, they think that she must be the reason it happened.

We always like to imagine that our own feelings and behaviour are beyond reproach and that if we are stung to anger or complaint it is for a very good reason. When approaching the pain and the difficulties that can be found in a blended family, you should not underestimate the role of your own less savoury or unacceptable feelings, such as envy and jealousy. Paul, now twenty-six, is probably more aware than his mother of her feelings towards her ex-husband and his new partner.

> Children within a relationship need to understand that their parents will be feeling the same as them – jealous, guilty, hurt, etc. It took me quite a long time to understand that though my mother likes my father, she is jealous and upset to see him enjoying a level of relationship with his new partner that she would like herself. Her hurt is not caused by Deirdre, but by seeing a situation she wants, one that she also envies friends for having, except that the involvement of an ex-husband probably makes it more extreme. It seems to me that rather than falling into the trap of seeing your happiness or theirs as more important (that is, you as a child and them as parents), you should try to reach a situation where the obvious (that is, your

happiness is dependent to some degree on theirs) can be recognized and discussed.

Sue, in her late forties and divorced from her husband when their children were toddlers, felt a bit threatened when he found a new partner after living alone for some years.

It all became a bit different when Shirley arrived. Obviously I'd not begrudge Jim his happiness, and his having a girlfriend didn't make him in any way 'unfit' to see his own children. Besides, Shirley is a nice person and quite reminds me of myself in the sort of role she plays in their relationship. I must say now that I would have been most upset if she had tried to become their real stepmother. Legally, I mean. I suppose she did become that by way of living with Jim as his wife in all but the legal sense. If she had tried to do something like that, my attitude towards her would have been very different. In my sort of situation, trying to make someone else's children your own only really makes sense if your ex is unfit to be a parent in some way. Even then it would have to be something that made them dangerous to the children before I'd consider it. Funnily enough, it's not the family set-up that caused me the most problems but watching the man I used to live with enjoying the sort of lifestyle with a partner that I'd like for myself with someone of my own.

Emma, now twenty, lives with her father, who does not have a permanent partner. Her mother does, and Emma was very aware of his reactions to this.

It was all a bit unfair, because the things we did when I went to stay at my mother's made it seem so idyllic, and then I'd return home and I think my father got jealous. This wasn't because he didn't do things with me – holidays with him were great until I hit adolescence just like a 'normal' kid. His jealousy was because he envied my mother and her man for their happiness. It didn't seem to be an envy founded in the idea of the 'other man', but rather because it was a lifestyle he wanted and here was somebody who could have been part of it come back to tell him what a great time she has had. My mother and father never seemed to talk things over, to the extent that though they like each other, my mother thinks he is a pain in the arse and he thinks she is selfish in terms of her general lifestyle.

The existence of the children is an unavoidable consideration from the very beginning of a new relationship. You can start off badly simply because privacy and the opportunity to be alone together can be hard to find, and you would be superhuman if you did not resent this. When Philip and Carol began to get close, she had to accept that his children were just as important as she was.

The kids were very high on his list of priorities when they were younger, so it meant we didn't go out or get time together alone. That was something you could understand if you are their parent. I was not a parent at the time, I was a young, single girl. Even the responsibility of making enough food to go round was something I found very hard. You've got to learn to demand a great deal less and accept a great deal more. I wasted a lot of energy worrying and getting uptight because we couldn't go out or because I hadn't been alone with Philip for weeks. Whenever you went into the house, there were people.

Christine similarly felt that her partner Gregory's three children from his former marriage had to be included.

> It probably helped that his last girlfriend didn't like children and they never really got on with her. What had happened was that Gregory had always had fort-nightly weekend access to the children and he and his girlfriend organized their lives so that she was away when they came or that he went away with the kids. It seemed like a strange set-up to me as an outside ob-server. It wasn't for me at all, since I thought that the kids should be part and parcel of the whole set-up.
>
> This was part of my decision about him. When we got together, it was very much that we were going to be a family, albeit on a fortnightly basis. I come from a big family and so like having children around.

What is good for the parents may not necessarily be so for the children, and vice versa. Compromise is not easy to achieve, and in most cases either the new relationship loses out because of the effort made to keep the children happy and secure or the children suffer because so much energy is invested in the new marriage that their needs are neglected. All of us fulfil many roles at any one time in our lives. We are parents to our own children at the same time as being a child to our own parents; husbands and wives at the same time as being fathers and mothers. But the roles often conflict – who has not endured the awkwardness of being bossed around and coddled by their parents while trying to do exactly the same thing to their own progeny? The clash between roles often leads to arguments and tension within a conventional family, and the likelihood of conflict is even greater when roles that do not usually coincide do so. Not many people expect to be in the midst of a new love affair at the same time as becoming a mum or a dad.

You may also begin badly if one of the adults has never before had any real contact with children. You are not born knowing how to be a parent, it is something you pick up by watching how your parents do it and then by practical experience with your own children. New step-parents may find themselves facing a stepchild who has every reason to want to be critical, and who is old enough and articulate enough to be able to notice and comment on the step-parent's inability and uncertainty. In this society we seem to place an unreasonable emphasis on adult knowledge and infallibility. We frown on the idea of an adult saying to a child, 'I haven't the foggiest idea!' So you are likely to feel that you ought to know what you are doing and to collapse in an agony of self-recrimination, or explode in anger, if a child belittles you. Carol, taking on Philip's four children when she was in her twenties, remembers:

> I think the children weren't exactly sure from first off how to react to me. I was more their age group than their parents, which ultimately has done us all a big favour. They were a little fazed, but on the other hand they're quite generous and open-minded. There was a little bit of jealousy here and there, and a few bad feelings. But this was just because they were not very mature and didn't know what to do. I wasn't very mature either, so I had to make it up as I went along as well.

The age not only of the new partner but of the children themselves can have some effect on your feelings about them, and your role. Carol thinks that

> if you are a young adult, you can be badly confused by children due to your lack of knowledge. You would be happier with the twelve to fifteen age group. It's a

combination, and it depends on the adult involved and on their tastes and personality and those of the children. There are no hard and fast rules. Theoretically younger children are easier, but I've met people who have been driven into the trees by a five-year-old.

Parenting in a different style from that which the child has known may provoke arguments. Children may resist because they feel they are losing the stability that comes with knowing that their way is the way. The problem is that all of us fall back on childish patterns when we are under stress, and you too may need to cling to the conviction that you are right. Fiona, with two children of her own, had her partner Dave's two daughters from his previous marriage to stay every weekend. She and the elder girl were on bad terms for some time.

There is this ad on television that I can't watch without blushing, all to do with a roll of lavatory paper and a young girl. In the first couple of years of our marriage I had a running battle with Dave's daughter about lavatory rolls. It was perfectly ridiculous and I honestly don't know why it started or why it became so important. When I change a roll, I always put it so the free edge is at the back towards the wall. I'd go in and find she'd changed it round. So I would change it and so would she. Then I'd go in and find she'd given it such a tug that the whole roll had unravelled and was lying in a heap, and I'd go and scream at her for being so wasteful. And she'd scream at me for being stupid and we wouldn't speak to each other for days. I can't remember when it stopped being important, and I can't even remember whether we do it my way or hers now. I think it doesn't matter, and it just depends on who puts the new one in the bog. But at the time, it was ridiculously important and I'd love to know why.

If you have problems, it is very easy to blame this entirely on the fact that you are a blended family. Many people in this situation have a degree of anxiety about the way they see the children's behaviour, which is not borne out or shared by others, such as teachers, who deal with the children. You may believe that what are actually typical disagreements between a parent and a child or adolescent are a problem and a consequence of the blended family experience. You can even make it worse for yourself because of this misinterpretation. Instead of shrugging with an 'all kids do this' attitude, you may worry excessively about your inadequacies or complain bitterly about the children's short-comings. For example, all children will be rude or cheeky at times and will resist ordinary requests to do chores such as making beds or laying tables. In a 'normal' family such behaviour should, and usually would, get short shrift. In a blended family you may allow them to get away with it, making excuses for them because of the circumstances or because you feel unable to enforce a request. Temporary and natural bolshiness will sometimes touch such a raw nerve, that you explode in a rage that is inappropriate to the actual 'offence'.

A step-parent can have a sense of guilt, failure and even of being evil if he or she does not love a new partner's children. One way of dealing with this dissatisfaction with yourself is to 'project' it on to the child concerned. Projection is when we take our own 'bad' feelings about a thing or person and dump them on it or them instead. We may be angry with or jealous of a child, but think that it is quite monstrous that we should harbour such strong, destructive feelings about an innocent, harmless, little object. But the feelings still exist, so we tell ourselves that perhaps the child really deserves them, perhaps it is the child who is the monster, not us. In an attempt to protect ourselves we then see evil, calculation and viciousness in everything the child does. This is why we sometimes get upset about only one child. Having become a scapegoat and having acquired the label of being 'bad', a child may decide that he or she has no choice but to behave badly and live up to that role.

We can easily forget that parents in a conventional family argue and disagree with their own children, and do not always find their behaviour acceptable. We never think to ask or wonder whether we 'get on' with our own children yet we often agonize about how we fit in with children in a blended family. No parents love their children all the time, and you should not demand more of yourself as a step-parent than you would as a birth parent. Furthermore, the step-relationship has an important difference in that you may find you take on the responsibility that goes with being a parent without being given the power. Deirdre and Paul seemed to get on for the first eleven years they knew each other, but had a serious and long disagreement when he was eighteen.

I think all those years of tension under the surface flared up in the year he left school. He took a year off before university. All through sixth-form college he had talked about hitching to the East and so forth. In the event, he went to France for two weeks, picking grapes, and then let his grandfather get him a job in an office. We were furious. We both let him know we were really disappointed in his lack of enterprise, and that we thought he was wasting his time and his opportunities. James had a few tense and unsatisfactory phone calls with him in that time, but I hardly spoke to him for months.

Then I suddenly realized what a total, selfish beast I was being. I was taking out on him the fact that I felt a type of responsibility for him and what happened to him in life, but had no way of influencing him. I was acting like a mother by demanding – but not by communicating. I never really asked him to tell me why he'd done this. When I did, he had a good reason. I wrote and apologized and, bless him, he forgave me. We've got on much better since then and we talk now. He opens up to us a good deal more than he did.

You may find an additional stress that is unique to a restructured family. It is common for children and their parents to have disagreements. When one parent and a particular child are at loggerheads, the other parent may play mediator and heal the breach. If the birth parents are in different households, however, this is less likely to occur, even if they have retained a civilized contact. The resultant, and often continuing, ill feeling can affect everyone in both families. Sue's two boys have lived with her since she divorced her husband, Jim, when they were very young. She felt she had to stand back if an argument arose between the children and their father.

Jim and one of the boys went through a bad patch when they didn't really talk much. I think having your kids around but not really there all the time is a very lucky situation – a lot of pleasure and not much pain, if you get my meaning. This situation was the only real time my relationship with Jim and Shirley was in danger of becoming quite sour. Mark was eighteen and definitely old enough to sort it out himself, but it was very hard to let him do it. I was his mother, but I wasn't Jim's partner any more, so I found myself biting my lip quite often. Even though I could tell Mark what part of his life I thought was causing the problem, I couldn't really influence it. It was important to me to maintain contact, and I liked them both anyway. It was just the way they behaved and the fact that because I had been a full-time parent I couldn't behave in that way myself and thought it was something Jim shouldn't do either.

Disciplining children is one of the most controversial and difficult areas of parenting in a conventional family, and it can be doubly so in a reconstituted one. We so often judge whether we are doing the job of parenting properly by whether or not we could be said to be in charge and in control. Children know this, and in a situation where challenge and conflict are to be expected will sense and use any adult uncertainty. You may find yourself under twin, conflicting demands, both unrealistic: to be soft on them because they have already suffered so much, and to be hard on them because you do not want to be accused of not being a proper parent. It may be particularly hard for step-parents to impose discipline if they bring to the relationship a lack of self-esteem accompanied by a lack of self-confidence. This could be further complicated by their not being sure of their right to discipline children who are not their own.

To understand why discipline is such a problem for stepfamilies, you have to understand what discipline is for in any family. Perhaps the main purpose, which is usually quoted when you ask parents why they need to have control over their children, is to protect young people from doing anything that could hurt them. This may cover anything from preventing crawling babies from sticking their fingers into electric sockets to keeping teenagers in after dark so they will not be led astray. Delve a bit deeper and you will realize that the second, more important function is to teach them manners and self-control – to socialize them and prepare them to be acceptable members of the community.

But all theory aside, the real, immediate and arguably the most necessary reason for discipline is to stop them from doing something that drives you scatty.

As a step-parent in a blended family you may have confused and conflicting views on this topic. Whether you admit it or not, you might be ambivalent about their coming to harm. All parents have moments when they would like the ground to open up and swallow their children. In most blended families this wish is less easy to admit to because it is often genuinely desired. Since at some time or other most step-parents have horrible fantasies about their stepchildren being hurt or even being 'removed', when danger threatens they may react with extra fear and rage. This is another form of 'projection' – the reality may be too uncomfortably close to what you have secretly, guiltily, wished for. So you dump your anger at yourself on to the child who almost caused it to happen.

If you are an adult in a blended family, you may desperately want it to appear 'normal' and hope the children will not let you down. You will probably forget that in a conventional family parents and their children frequently clash, and feel that any situation where you appear not to be in control underlines the fact that yours is not an ordinary, happy family. Miriam married Edward eleven years ago and found herself the weekend parent of three young children.

> They were little monsters when they were young, always trying to make a fool of me, especially in public. I hated taking them to the supermarket and would go to any lengths to make sure I was stocked up for their visits, rather than have to go there with them in tow. They'd snatch things off shelves and go sulky or have a crying fit if I didn't buy them sweets. I'd

cram things into bags at the checkout with these grizzling kids kicking the trolley and feel *everyone* was looking at me, knowing that they weren't mine and I was making a total mess of bringing them up.

But the main problem is that, if you are not the birth parent in your blended family, these children may drive you mad just by being. The demands you make of them could well be unrealistic and you may be seeing indiscipline and the need for a stern hand when what could be normal, harmless childhood behaviour requires nothing more than tolerance. It is not their behaviour that drives you up the wall – it is their very existence.

Whether or not you think your blended family is a success and whether or not you are comfortable within it may largely depend, on the surface, on your sex. Being a stepmother may seem easier than being a stepfather, because in this society the role of a mother is better defined than that of a father. It can therefore be simpler for a woman to go through the motions of what everyone thinks of as mothering, and be accepted by herself and other adults as doing the job properly. This can carry the seeds of its own destruction, however, if the children involved become resentful of what they see as attempts to take over the 'real' mother's role. When this happens, a stepmother may feel particularly rejected and hurt because in her eyes she has been doing her best to give the children what she thinks they need. To discover where this goes wrong, it is necessary to examine, as we do in the next chapter, the children's feelings.

It is noteworthy that most step-parents are fathers but that the greatest disquiet at what is happening within a blended family is usually expressed by the women involved, largely because it is the women who tend to be left to cope with the family while the man absents himself physically and often emotionally to fulfil his role as breadwinner. Fewer stepmothers than natural mothers have paid employment, which means that they make a greater effort to be like 'real' mothers than real mothers do, and release the man from some responsibilities. He can play a smaller part in the blended family than he might have otherwise if a parental presence is fully met by his non-working partner. As well as providing a physical presence, the mother figure shoulders the burden of the emotional matters within the family, even if the children are his.

Whichever adult is the parent of the children involved in a blended family and whatever the living or visiting arrangements, it is often the woman who looks after them, not the man. When children from a first marriage are sent to 'see Dad in his new family', this usually means that the new wife or partner has to take care of them, sometimes without anyone asking about her views. Miriam felt that she took on far more responsibility for her partner Edward's children than he did.

Edward just never seemed to understand that my feelings about having his children to stay were very different to his. Of course, it was easy for him. They'd arrive on a Sunday and he'd spend the day playing with them and just when he was beginning to feel bored or at the end of his patience, it was Monday morning and he could go off to work. He could then end the visit on Saturday with another round of fun and games, and the fact that in the middle I'd had to look after and amuse them from seven in the morning until eight at night, on my own, was conveniently forgotten. I will never, ever, forget the day, pregnant with Zoe who is our second child, Edward came and told me that his ex's doctor had said she must have a rest and the children were coming for a week. 'Oh,' I said, 'you said no, of course?' 'Of course not,' he said. 'I'm picking them up tomorrow morning.' I was speechless, but the only reason they didn't actually land on me that week was that I was taken to hospital the next day with a threatened miscarriage. If I'd just been weak, ill and run off my feet, I'd have had to have coped.

That the onus is on the woman may, not unreasonably, cause deep resentments and conflict. This is probably why it is generally the women who worry about what is happening within the family and therefore have feelings of guilt and inadequacy while the men have a rosier view.

The truth is that all families are imperfect, and you probably need to expect less of yourself and forgive more. Establishing and continuing a blended family is likely to be hard work, but enormously rewarding. You may not realize quite how much any problems that arise are caused not by the actual situation but by your emotions and interpretations of what is going on. In order to chart a safe and happy course through the possible pitfalls, you need to recognize and explore your own feelings, and those of the other people involved. You, being the adult, will bear the responsibility for what happens in the new family and it is up to you to keep trying, but you can succeed only if you understand how and why children react the way they do.

5

The Child's View

We have looked at how and why the adults in a blended family may feel and react the way they do. As you can see, what is going on openly may not be easy to comprehend or cope with unless you have looked a little bit deeper into the complex mix of emotions under the surface. If this is true for the adults concerned, it is even more true for the children. Although you may not have chosen to break up your original relationship, you might have some control of the new one, whereas children have no say in the ending or starting of their parents' relationships. The only power they have lies in showing you their dissatisfaction. They can do this with a frightening effectiveness but frequently with very little insight. If your blended family is to have some success and if you are to help the children involved, you will need to understand how they are feeling and why.

The myth of the wicked step-parent is one that most children have heard and may readily embrace when they find themselves entering a blended family, though this myth has nothing to do with stepmothers, stepfathers or stepbrothers and stepsisters. It has come about as a coping technique to allow children to make sense of the different aspects of their personalities and reactions to their own parents.

As they grow, children discover that the loving, caring mother can also be the punitive, angry mother. The child can sometimes love all embracingly, but also hate equally powerfully. Before young children can integrate these opposites and accept they can exist side by side, they 'solve' the paradox by projecting all the bad aspects outside. So, when a story tells of the saintly mother who dies and is replaced by the wicked stepmother, this is in fact a reflection of what the child feels happens when Loving Mother disappears and is replaced by Angry Mother. Eventually children grow up to a point where they recognize that someone can be angry with them and go on loving them at the same time, and that they can do the same.

This separation of different parts of yourself and of your parents is a valuable part of development. We need such devices to give us time to understand ourselves and our emotions. A problem arises, however, when we take them literally. If the story is accepted unquestioningly by children and adults and used to project their anger, grief or confusion on to the death of a relationship or the beginning of a new one, it does not help them to resolve uncomfortable feelings. Instead, it prolongs them. It is far more comfortable to think not that you harbour a nasty wish to destroy another person but that he or she is a monster who is somehow responsible for all the bad things that are happening.

Most young people fantasize that they are not their parents' real child at some time during childhood, especially in adolescence. If you are alienated from the rest of the family or angry with someone inside it is quite normal to indulge in a daydream about being the foundling child of a rich or royal family who one day will reclaim you and take you away. It provides a way of coming to terms with the fact that you may hate and be angry with the people responsible for you at the same time as loving them deeply. Children in a blended family, however, have the fantasy come true. While in a first-time family children have to learn to deal with their mixed feelings, children in a blended family may never have to reconcile their anger or disagreements with the adult in authority with the recognition that the adult loves them. In the former, children eventually get over their bitterness; in the latter it may remain with them and form a permanent barrier.

These feelings are by no means confined to the children concerned. In recent years there has been a rash of popular films and books that portray children as possessed or evil. These represent the other side of the wicked stepmother myth, and they can reassure adults that they may be right to consider the troublesome child a deliberate and conscious schemer. If you assume this, however, you and the child may both set off on the wrong foot. You would see a deliberate campaign or entrenched attitudes when there are none, and also condemn the child as 'knowing' and 'bad' when he or she is probably just as confused as you are.

Problems with a child sometimes start during or immediately after the break-up of the original relationship. Children can be truly awful to the parent left in charge because they recognize that he or she will stand and take it. Tantrums, depression and accusations against the remaining parent for having caused the break-up or driven away the errant parent are common. The child will often make things worse by insisting that the absent parent is some sort of saint and has to be treated gently. This is wholly understandable, because the child has a fund of pain, anger and fear that has to be expended somewhere, but dare not focus this on the parent who has departed for fear that it would provoke a further withdrawal. After all, have they not already proved that they can and will leave? At the same time the child's unfair behaviour can be deliberately provocative. The fact that one parent has gone brings the horrible suspicion that the other might too. So in trying your patience to the limits, the child is testing you to see if you will throw up your hands and walk away.

Children may come to appreciate the blended family and new step-relations, but for a large number it is a stressful and difficult arrangement in which they have very few choices. A central point for children in a blended family is that loss of some form must always be involved. They will have lost one parent and the sense of being in a secure family. They will have experienced a loss of innocence that is related not to sexuality but to the comfortable feeling that all is right with the world because Dad and Mum love them and will always be there. After any loss there can be feelings of guilt, anger, remorse and mourning, and the lost person may be idealized. Since this wonderful person has abandoned the children, this may in turn lead to their having a lower sense of their own worth.

It is important to remember that children cannot help but be selfish and egocentric. Hardly any relationships break up because one or other partner decides that he or she no longer wants to be a parent – they break up because the two adults find they can no longer sustain their relationship. But children do not see it that way. They do not see that the husband-and-wife relationship is no longer satisfying. They think that Mum or Dad has got tired of them. While you may be struggling with the idea of failure because you are wondering whose fault it was that your relationship ended, the child too senses failure and wonders what he or she did to lose the other parent's love. When a new partner comes along, all of these fears and worries may be directed by the child against this adult. Children may want to gather up their resentment and bitterness and heap them on the out-sider. They may also want to test the newcomer. If the birth parent, who owes them more allegiance and love than a stranger, can turn his or her back and walk away, will this person not be even more likely to give up if life becomes difficult? The child, feeling rejected and abandoned, may want to push the new partnership to the limit to see if the new adult will also conclude the child is unworthy and unlovable. When Michael's mother died and his father, Marty, married Sheila, Michael reacted badly. Michael is at boarding-school and every time he visits there seems to be trouble. Sheila suspects he is doing it deliberately.

> Marty used to be endlessly patient, but now he's just fed up. Whenever there's a new quarrel – every time he comes home Michael is at the centre of some new row – Marty now just rolls his eyes to heaven and says, 'What do you expect?' I think the worst part of it is that I simply can't see what Michael gets out of it. It doesn't seem to give him any satisfaction. In fact, I've caught him once or twice crying, and I think he does this more than any of us realize. But he won't talk about it. In fact, he won't *talk* about anything.

It might help if you can accept right at the beginning that children in a blended family by and large do not like being in this position. In their eyes they have little or nothing to gain by co-operating. Appealing to their better natures or saying 'Look at how much happier this relationship is making your father/mother' carries no weight with them. Children are obviously able to see when you are happy or miserable, but are less able to understand what causes those emotions and what relevance their behaviour has to this. Children may feel guilty or bad, and even hold themselves responsible for your misery. But at the same time they do not believe that their own behaviour could have any effect on the new relationship. They often look at it only from their own perspective and see themselves as the losers. Children are not consulted about the breakdown of the original relationship, and are not offered a compromise, yet in the new family compromise is likely to be the first thing they are asked for. So why should the children co-operate or even understand what is being asked of them?

Children are rarely 'better off' without the missing parent. However badly they may have suffered, and may still be suffering, at the hands of the missing parent, they will still love them. You will need to remember that while love of a partner for a partner may die, the link between parent and child is for life. To you, a 'parent' is the person who does the job – looking after the children and consistently being there when required, as well as providing food, clean clothes, a house and earning the money to make this possible. When another adult takes over responsibility for these practical matters, you may feel that he or she deserves to be given the regard and respect due a parent. But to the child, 'parent' is an identity. Even when that person no longer takes care of the day-to-day details, he or she is still a parent. Above all, what a parent is has more to do with the child's identity than the parent's role. If the one who has left ceases to be a parent, a part of the child's own identity will be lost. Deirdre remembers seven-year-old Paul voicing a worry he had obviously been brooding over.

> James would sit with him at bedtime, reading or chatting. One night, Paul apparently asked, 'If Laura marries again, will you still be my dad?' That touched him. 'Yes,' he promised, 'I'll *always* be your father.'

The new parent may be particularly resented if either adult tries to paint the absent parent as 'bad'. Even if by anyone's standards this may be true, you must appreciate how this might strike the children. Since part of their own identity comes from that parent, accepting the parent who is no longer there as wicked, and the time they spent together as a mistake, is the same as having to accept that they themselves are partly wicked and partly a mistake.

Unquestioning loyalty is something that a child will invest in a parent whether it is asked for, earned or justified.

Children in blended families may find that their loyalties are split. Do not forget that although you may have known the ex-partner for a small part of your life, the child has known this adult for all his or her life. Children will most probably feel intensely disloyal if asked to turn their backs on the missing parent, and may be angry at one birth parent for criticizing the other. You may think you have perfectly justifiable reasons for denigrating this adult, but the children will feel such remarks are being directed against themselves as well. Remember, too, that a person can have failings as a partner and still be a good parent. And that even though you may not think he or she fulfils the role of father or mother, the child may have other standards.

In many cases children decide, either on their own or with encouragement from the other parent, that the abandoning parent has let them down and should be rejected, and then refuse all contact. But you will be sadly mistaken if you think this is a clean break and that lack of contact does not harm or mark the child in any way. Conlan is twenty-three and at university, and his parents split up when he was twelve. His mother has remained on her own while his father has married the girlfriend he met soon after leaving.

My brother and I had very different reactions when my dad left. I was three years older, so maybe I could understand it a bit better. I mean, I don't want to say that anyone was to blame; I know it wasn't my mum's fault. They hadn't been happy for a long time and you've got to see that there are two sides to this sort of thing, aren't there? He and his girlfriend get on OK and I'm sure it was the right thing for him. I used to go and see them a lot, and when I was seventeen I went and lived with them for my last year at school and my year off before I went to college. But my brother wouldn't talk to him and wouldn't see him. I think Mum was quite pleased about this, because she always saw it as me letting her down and him seeing things clearly and being on her side. I don't think she's been so pleased the last few years, though. I'll be finishing my degree in a couple of months and I should get a good one. I've got a job lined up and Gill, my girlfriend, and I are talking of getting married. My life's pretty sorted out. My brother's been in and out of trouble since he left school at sixteen. He moves around from one casual job to the next and doesn't seem able to settle at anything. He's got a violent streak in him, too, and tends to pick fights when he's been on the drink – and that's often.

Children have a right to retain workable links with both their birth parents just as much as the parent has a right to a new partner, which means that compromise, with adults getting what they need and the children getting what they need, is what has to be worked towards. The most important thing to recognize is that children are separate people, not merely an extension of their parents. Both parents and children can want and need something that is not only different but may be conflicting. Rather than one getting what he or she wants and the other losing out, the trick is to identify what the various priorities are and then to negotiate towards a position where both can be satisfied.

In some broken families the remaining parent and the children build up a special relationship. Paul, whose parents, James and Laura, separated when he was one, lived with his mother until going to university at the age of nineteen.

I've lived with my mother, so obviously I'm very close

to her in a way that I think is different to other two-parent children. This can be a little cloying at times, but on the whole I think it's valuable and certainly not a childhood that, in retrospect, I would have had any other way. If it suits the people who are really involved, then you should be glad, feel lucky or special. You probably have more interesting experiences, fun and love than if you had stayed as part of a 'normal' family – especially if your real parents had stayed together 'for your sake'. In this way I think family life itself is at fault with its 'first love, only love' myth and the idea that divorce is failure. Obviously, social norms are not going to change overnight, but a re-examination of the rhetoric and the reality is long overdue. You have to start by doing it yourself.

Sometimes a child simply enjoys the sole attention of the parent, playing games, having private jokes, and they spend much undivided time together. In other cases the child is leaned on quite heavily by the adult for emotional or practical support. Children may then take on what they see as adult or even parental responsibilities. When a new partner comes along, although the parent may be aware that the children are missing out because more attention and time are given to the new partner than to them, he or she may expect the children to be relieved at having responsibilities beyond their years once more lifted from their shoulders. In fact, as already mentioned in Chapter 3, children often resent being replaced, and in their eyes the new adult becomes a substitute and a rival not only for the missing parent but also for them.

Rivalry may emerge from other quarters in a blended family. The step-parent may have their own children, and no matter who lives where, there are likely to be difficulties.

Children may live with the new partnership or visit for weekends. The step-parent's children too may live there permanently or visit for weekends. As time goes on, there may even be new children of the partnership, and the estranged partners of the central couple may have new relationships and children, adding half-brothers and half-sisters and further stepchildren.

In all these cases, each child may experience jealousy and guilt. They may be jealous of the children who are seen to occupy as much of their original parent's time and attention, or even more, than they do. And they may be guilty if they have taken a central role in the life of the new step-parent and they can see the step-parent's child losing out.

Even if the adults concerned are making the transition quite easily, the tug of loyalty in the children may cause enormous conflict within them, which may be severe enough to produce signs of stress if it is not recognized and dealt with. Children in blended families often go back to babyish, disruptive behaviour that you might have thought they had grown out of. Children of any age may revert to bedwetting or having temper tantrums, or to clinging and whining behaviour that demands attention.

There may be a dramatic split in the way they conduct themselves inside and outside the home. Some children show their unhappiness only at home and are perfectly normal at school or with other relatives and friends. Some appear perfectly normal when they are with their parents but raise hell in school or outside, often to the total surprise and astonishment of the parents when they find out.

Difficulties are often made worse because the young person does not tell anyone outside the family what is happening or how they feel about it. The child may be ashamed of being 'different' and so not want to reveal the change in circumstances at home, or, if this itself is no secret, their own reactions. Marvin, whose father left when he was eleven, says:

> At the time my dad left you get sort of embarrassed about it at that age, so I didn't tell anyone at school. My friends only knew when they didn't see my dad about much. Only my best friend knew about it at the time. There was no explicit 'I need a shoulder to cry on' sort of thing, but just the fact that I still had a best friend was good. There were others, and if I had been older, I think I would have talked about it. But in first year at secondary school it wasn't something that it occurred to you to talk about to other people in the same situation. Later on, you meet lots of people like yourself. My friend is in a stepfamily as well now. His mum has just remarried and he tells me there are occasional problems. I can give advice because I understand as the same things happen to me.

This can obviously lead to problems if outsiders, such as teachers, make unfair judgements on what they see as unexplained and unreasonable moodiness and lack of concentration.

The bad behaviour typical of children in blended families can often be divided into two broad areas – harm to others, where the anger and confusion are turned against the outside world, and harm to themselves, where it is turned inwards. Examples of the first could be bullying at school and vandalism. Examples of the second could be playing truant from school, doing badly in their work or, in slightly older children, taking risks by sleeping around, using drugs or joyriding. Some children may even turn to self-mutilation, cutting themselves or having tattoos put on by schoolfriends or professionals. In young adult years there may be hasty marriage, often followed by divorce. Girls from blended families often express a desire to marry early. Boys often say they intend not to marry at all or not to have children of their own.

Children's confused feelings can make it even harder for them to accept the new partner. If the replacement turns out to be someone they can and do like, they may have a sense of guilt. The more they find themselves drawn to and liking the replacement for their own parent, the more torn and hostile they may become. Their guilt at allowing the new parent to take the place of the old makes the children angry with themselves and also with the new partner and the other parent, on behalf of the one who is being replaced. Children may start to act out what they see as a parent's role, by leaving or refusing to have contact with one parent or by making demands that seem inappropriate. In effect, they are playing the divorcing or divorced role to show loyalty to one parent or to punish the other. Philip has kept in close contact with his four children, one of whom moved in with him and his second wife, Carol, soon after they were married. This son had a row with his mother and at times does not want to get in touch with her. Philip himself has little contact with her, and thinks

> there was always a feeling on her part that I was saying, 'Keep away from her', but that couldn't have been further from the truth. You can't push anyone into a situation where they don't want to be any more.

Carol felt it was important that the boy

> kept a relationship of some sort with his mother. I used to insist at one stage, but there came a time when he was old enough to make up his own mind. You can't stand over them with a shotgun.

> You should never forget that when a family divides, there

are people on either side and there is always someone in the middle. Inevitably the person in the middle acts as a buffer and may be crushed between the two colliding forces or trampled underfoot as you continue the battle. If you must take a side, it would be much better to view the child as a bridge – a means of making and continuing contact. Better still would be for both of you to get on the same side, or at least not to include the child in your conflict. Matthew lives with his father and his second wife, Marian, in preference to being with his mother and sister. He feels his mother, father and Marian get on fairly well, but that even if they did not, it should not involve him.

> I like both of them. That is my business, not theirs, and if they don't like each other, that's their business, not mine. As long as they don't try to include me in any of their little fights, I'm happy. I think I find myself not wanting to be involved in any fights and keep out of them a lot.

Emma, who lives with her father and sees her mother and boyfriend regularly, resents being in the middle of their fights.

> My main gripe would have to be that at this time my parents' problems seemed to come to a head and instead of dealing with them between themselves, I was made a sort of message-bearer. They'd talk a bit on the phone, but I think their characters sort of stopped them from achieving anything that way. Perhaps they should have had more access to each other rather than to me! I'm sure you can imagine the scenario – 'your mother this', 'your father that', etc., with me in the middle beginning to despise them both while I still loved them both. This was a really twisting time. It was very strange because

it was *their* problem, not mine, so it didn't seem to me to fit the normal stepfamily problem scenario. There's often so much focus on the children that you forget what I now accept, that adults are just children with bigger bodies and more experience and responsibilities, but with basically the same needs.

It is hardly surprising that the children themselves may encourage conflict, given the high level of conflicting feelings they are experiencing. Many take advantage of the lack of communication to play parents off against each other, or to try to turn parent against step-parent. Some children in a blended family may be egged on by others in the same position or themselves realize the opportunities for emotional blackmail. The familiar cry of 'But Mum lets me stay up late' or 'Dad says he'll buy it for me' may often be used by the child to get extra privileges or treats, and parental competitiveness is common. What the child gains is always a substitute for what he or she wants, however, which is attention and proof of love. Once started, this competition is rarely won by anyone, because what the child needs is not obtained through this medium.

A child or young person cannot help but feel left out as a parent carries on a love affair with a new partner. It must be remembered that youngsters find sex intriguing but look upon the idea of their parents having sex lives as hilarious, ridiculous or disgusting. In a conventional family, by the time they are old enough to be interested in sexual activity it is usually a settled, comfortable exchange that goes on between parents without children consciously noticing. In a blended family it is sometimes all too visible, which may have unfortunate consequences. Children may express their unease and revulsion at the parents' 'carrying on'. They may feel driven to compete with the parent, by having their own sexual relationships or by flirting with the parent's partner, if of the opposite sex, or a stepbrother or stepsister if there is one. The child may also flirt with the missing parent, either as a way of keeping and not losing them too, or as a way of competing with the parent who has failed to do so. While open sexual behaviour is obviously more likely to be the route taken by teenagers, it can appear in even younger children. Tragically, it often leads to sexual abuse, premature sexual activity and unwanted or unplanned pregnancy.

The day-to-day workings of a blended family can produce many difficulties for the young people concerned. Step-parent and stepchild might have radically different values. Birth parent and child can clash, but this is not usually because you have different beliefs. After all, children get most of their value systems from their own parents. Most disagreements are about independence and responsibility and are a means by which children, even those of a very young age, can assert their right to stand alone. When the dust settles, more children share beliefs and ideas with their parents than have strong differences. However, in a blended family adult and child can certainly have a very different set of values and young children may be surprisingly protective about these. Added to the importance of standing up and defending your values to prove you can rebel against your parents – something all children have to do – may be the need to defend yourself and by extension the missing parent from a take-over by the new partner. This can lead to vicious and entrenched arguments about trivial things. The argument that is raging is hardly ever about the specific item that is being contested.

Whether or not relationships within a blended family are harmonious, the new arrangement will bring about many changes in the household, which can be very unsettling for all involved. For the parent, having a new partner move in, moving into his or her household or acquiring a new place for all of you is bound to be exciting and welcome. You may want the children to share this, but the chances are they will not. Even the joy of getting a new house or treats that have long been promised – space to have a pet, a room of their own or a garden – may be overshadowed by the loss of familiar surroundings and having to share the house with people they have not chosen to live with. If a new partner is moving in with them, children may feel their territory has been invaded and their security compromised. Adults may be happy to leave a home once shared with another partner – a partner they now wish to distance themselves from – while the child may want to retain that last link with the missing parent or the missing life that may be seen as idyllically happy 'until you spoiled it'. A new home may also mean that children lose touch with friends and neighbours, who may have become all the more important in a time of instability. They may equally 'lose' friends, even if you do not move house, if the new arrangements make them too ashamed or shy to bring their friends home any more.

Money may be in short supply in a blended family, particularly if one of the adults concerned is also having to maintain another household. This may result in a shortage of space if the family cannot afford the size of home it needs and everyone has to squeeze themselves into too small a space. Human beings, like all animals, have very strong feelings about the territory they inhabit. Children may feel that the house is no longer theirs and they do not belong, that they have been robbed of their privacy or status and that other members of the family have been given better conditions and more consideration than they have. Children these days are very aware of market forces and spending power is important to them. A tight budget may be yet another source of shame and discomfort to them, and they may blame it on being in a blended family.

Routines and schedules can give children a vital stability. Even those who have enjoyed a more flexible and bohemian lifestyle may react to the strains of a restructured family by wanting something more 'ordinary' and even boring, a demand that can be extremely irritating to their parents. Emma, now twenty, remembers going through a stage of wanting an alternative approach.

At the age of sixteen I suddenly found myself, much to my independently minded disgust, looking longingly at normal fathers returning to suburban house, loving wife and 2.3 children, even though this was a lifestyle I've never wanted and even despised.

Continuity is very reassuring to children. If you are combining two families, someone is necessarily going to have to accept change, which can obviously cause distress. As so often with these unhappy situations, however, you may be damned if you do and damned if you don't. If the new adult makes an effort to adopt the child's familiar routines and schedules as if they were his or hers too, the child may suspect the adult is cheating or being a phoney. If you do not lay down rules and, for example, let the children get away with not doing chores, they will not know where they stand and you may build up a store of resentment. Marvin saw some problems with 'house rules' when his mother's boyfriend moved in when he was thirteen and his sister ten.

My sister had problems getting on with Keith at first, probably because there had been a break of about three years without a man about the house. She's OK with him now that the ground rules are down. At the start, that was the big problem. For the first few months I don't think Keith ever laid down the law. But when he settled in and it started to become his house in a way, my sister would do something wrong and he'd have a go at her. She resented this. I think he's been there so long now that it's a case of if my sister doesn't like anything, then she's just got to put up with it.

What can be difficult for parents is realizing that their children have their own secret lives that are perfectly separate from the parents' lives. Something that is important to you is not to them, and vice versa. Something that is welcomed by you can be a tragedy to them, and vice versa. You may thus find yourself thoroughly confused and caught out sometimes when your child is simply not seeing an event in the same light as you are. For instance, you and your new partner may be eagerly anticipating and planning an anniversary that is special to you, and be totally puzzled at the child's ill temper that spoils an otherwise happy day. But from the child's point of view you may just be rubbing salt into the wound if he or she does not see the new partnership as something to celebrate. Similarly, there may be an anniversary that is meaningful to the children – such as the day they first realized their birth parents were splitting up – of which you are entirely ignorant. On, or approaching, that day you may be at a loss to understand why a child is so unhappy. Days that you think ought to be happy ones, such as birthdays or Christmas, may be extremely painful if the child is wanting to be with both parents and this is not possible.

It is often tempting to assume that a child is too young to comprehend what is going on, or to recognize the complexities of adult emotions. Emma, who was two when her parents separated, feels her ability to understand what was involved was not appreciated by her mother, who

seemed to have this idea that she was possessed of some sort of insight that I didn't have. I suppose all parents are like that, but it was as if she thought I wouldn't understand her or the concepts involved in a decayed adult relationship.

Matthew, aged seventeen, is scathing about the lack of respect for young people's ability to know what is happening in a failing or failed relationship.

I know lots of adults who think that children need 'to be told' about things like that. Children are not blind, they pick up on everything, good or bad.

Even at quite an early age young people are able to make reasoned judgements about adult relationships. Paul formed his own views of his parents' marriage, which ended when he was one.

I can see why they liked/like each other, but I can't envisage their relationship as a successful married one. Their personalities and approaches to life are very different. I'm glad they didn't 'stay together for the sake of the children'. I think that sort of attitude (unless there is a real need for two parents even if they are unhappy) is caused more by a desire to satisfy society. It's your and your children's life, the neighbours don't matter.

Very young children can often be extremely perceptive, and are sometimes even more so than adults. They have not yet learned to dissemble or forgotten how to tell the truth. Where adults may be fooled, perhaps because they want to accept the polite fictions of the white lie, a child may see straight through any evasion. Children can be quite refreshing in that they are direct about their feelings and let you know in no uncertain terms what they think, if you are prepared to listen. Face-to-face arguments can be better and easier to deal with than an adult's veiled insults and behind-your-back plotting. Carol remembers that

the older children were very outspoken, but that's easier. I'd rather have a good insult which is straight than a lot of mumbling or not speaking. You know then what you're fighting. The marvellous thing about a big family is that you are never going to be flavour of the month with everybody at once, but you are not going to be the total villain either. Two children can come to the decision that they are not going to have anything to do with you, but it's unlikely that all five will come to the same decision at the same time.

An adult may be put off explaining why a marriage is breaking up because the child's apparently naïve solution is that everyone can still go on living together. The reason is not that the child is too young to understand but that he or she does not necessarily want to understand. The child needs both of you, the child loves both of you, so why on earth can you not go on living together? As far as the child's needs are concerned, that is neither a silly question nor a ridiculous solution.

The age of any children at the time of a break-up obviously has a bearing on how they cope. Jack's parents split up ten years ago when he was seven. Both his parents now have stable relationships and Jack lives with his mother and her boyfriend. He is glad that, if they had to separate, they did so when he was still young.

I would have grown up thinking that they were most definitely my parents and nothing was ever going to break them up. If they had lasted until my teens, then it would have seemed as if they would last for ever. It would have freaked me out a lot more. Also, if the split had happened in my teens, then I would have got the impression that someone was trying to take over my dad's position. But because I never remember my dad as having a position in our family, he's not *family*, but just my dad. So I've got someone who replaced him physically, as it were, but not emotionally.

Emma's parents broke up when she was two.

I wasn't old enough to take it all in and worry about it. I didn't even know that I was supposed to worry. I have very little memory of the break-up, and this is a definite advantage. Children do notice the atmosphere of adult relationships around them, but I'm glad they split before I knew what was going on. I think that if it had happened at any other time, then sixteen to eighteen would have been the only other age where it could have been so easy. When you're that age you are already starting to want your independence. Obviously there would be problems, but not as bad as if you were say six or seven when you're aware but still very much dependent on your parents and you need emotional security. I feel sorry for kids that age whose parents split up, especially when the break is messy. Grown-ups can be so pathetic, too afraid to face the problems between themselves, so they use the children like a tug-of-war rope to work out their own frustrations.

How old the child is when the parent's new partner appears may also be important. Members of blended families, like any others, will always have their differences. There is no reason why new step-children should be instant fun and instantly lovable. And just because only one step-child out of several children reacts badly, you should not conclude it is the child rather than the situation. Children are likely to react in various ways depending on age, sex and personal history. Deirdre came along six years after Paul's parents had separated.

> Having a sort of stepmother has been a long-term experience. It's by no means right back to when I was too young to remember, but certainly long enough for it to feel it has always been like this. I think I was lucky that my parents split up before I knew what was going on. Obviously I missed out on any unpleasantness or upset surrounding the actual separation, but also I only knew my father alone or with the two girlfriends of his I actually met. Since Deirdre was/is the most long-term of these, I suppose you could say she was my stepmother. This was very easy to accept, because, even though I knew that he'd once been married to my mother, he and Deirdre had nearly always been together. I think that if I'd had to sit and watch James and my mother at the split, I might have had a rather more confused attitude about his relationship with Deirdre. The same would have been true if Deirdre had been part of a long line of women who spent time with my father.

The age of the step-parent can also affect how well the child and new adult get on. Jack's stepfather is in his late sixties and they share a house but very little else:

> My stepdad and I don't really get on and we basically stay clear of each other. I guess it's because he could almost be my grandad and he is very set in his ways – he doesn't like my hair and so on. It's age and culture clash, he could never replace my dad.

Perhaps one aspect of the difficulties experienced in a blended family is that adults assume and expect that a child is formed to a large part by them and conforms to their image of what children should be and how they should behave. Of course, it does not always happen like that because children have their own ideas. But at least adults watch their own children develop and often, without realizing it, adjust and adapt themselves accordingly. So when an already formed stepchild arrives, the average adult is uneasy. This child cannot be moulded in the same way as his or her own children, and indeed will often react against any attempt at such moulding. Frequently children display characteristics they inherit or copy from the other parent, and this can become a bone of contention. A child may find it immensely comforting to know he or she does something 'just like your dad/mum'. The new partner, however, may find it irritating or painful in its living reminder of the previous relationship.

The fault lies in how we view adult–child dynamics. We do not respect children as people. If we did and recognized they are individuals, not little copies of ourselves, we would all be better off. The relationship between a parent and child in our society is in many respects outrageous, and to be controlled in the way that even the most permissive of parents control their children is positively invasive. What often happens when a step-parent appears is that children, probably quite rightly, take the opportunity to revolt and say, 'You have absolutely no right to assume this kind of control over me.'

The imbalance of power between child and parent is shown by the fact that we call children by their names but they usually call us by our titles. What happens in the blended family is that this practice does not work. Adults are often most unhappy at the idea of children calling someone older than they are by a first name. This may be explained by saying it sounds rude or cheeky, as if the child were claiming a status, that of equal or friend, that we think they should not have. Strange, isn't it, that we feel uneasy when children claim the intimacy of friendship or equality with the very people with whom they should have the closest possible relationship?

Faced with their parents' partners in a new relationship, children are most unlikely to want to call them Dad or Mum, for all the reasons of resentment, jealousy and guilt that we have already discussed. They may wish to signal the reassessment of their relationships with their birth parents by calling them by their first names too. Emma lives with her father but sees her mother regularly. She feels that when she was a teenager her parents had a period of disagreeing and using her as a means of carrying on their arguments.

> This time in my life changed my attitude to my parents in a very concrete way, especially to my mother. Perhaps it would have been better if I'd moved in with her, but I think that would have scared everyone involved, especially her. She seemed to be very settled in a sort of lifestyle where she saw me as needing to be quite distant and not making too many emotional demands. This is reflected by the fact that she's 'Helen' and not 'Mum' now, whenever I talk to her or write. It's not a case of forgiving, just that the moment seems to be lost to get close to her and know her well, even though we are very similar in a lot of respects. It wasn't helped by my father's family, who, although they all like my mother, invariably side with my father, which makes me defend her. It's almost as if I feel or felt that they had no right to intervene in something that was between Dad, Helen and me. Thankfully, my mother's family are pretty distant and it was her that 'left' originally so I was spared it from both sides.

Children in blended families are quite likely to give some thought to the whole question of who you are, who they are and, as signified by these names and titles, what your relationship to each other is. Their conclusions may in some ways make for a better relationship but can cause discomfort to their parents because nothing is taken for granted. Paul considers that his relationship with his father is not quite the same as it would have been if they had lived together.

> My father and I saw each other quite regularly throughout my early life and, to be honest, when we didn't stay in contact as much as I'd have liked, it was probably a case of fifty-fifty on his and my part. I think it's more a part of his and my characters that we are not as close or in contact as much as we would like. I sometimes feel that he's more a friend than a 'significant' relative. To give an example of this, I'd probably listen to his advice, but if he told me to do something, I'd be less likely to comply than if my mother had told or asked me to do the same. I think in a way this makes him easier to deal with or to visit. At the times in my life that I've been most aware that he is my parent, I've quite often wanted to stay away. This might be due to the fact that I feel I'm being short-changed (therefore he's 'failing' me as a parent) or sometimes he gives me strong advice or criticism that I don't think is justified due to our level of contact. There is, of course, a chance that this reaction may be an excuse to ignore what I don't want to hear, but this isn't often the case. I've always tried to discourage the 'your father', 'your mother' comments that inevitably arise in this type of relationship.

Which surname a child is known by may become very important. Children may want to change their name if, for instance, they are living with a remarried mother and a stepfather and do not want to be singled out by having a different name from them. Alternatively, a child may cling against all the odds to a name conspicuously different from that of the rest of the family as a way of retaining a link with the absent birth parent. Some children choose to change their first names as a way of keeping a missing or dead parent alive.

Having looked at all the above issues, it seems appropriate to consider whether the children in a blended family present a special problem. When studied objectively and compared with other families, they are not found to be any more troublesome or troubled than children in natural families. But any problems between the children and adults in a restructured family are often put down to the step-relationship itself rather than to normal adult–child conflict. All children argue with their parents and all children can be sullen, graceless and rebellious at times, and especially during the teenage years. Most of it is not personal, and it is certainly not to do with being in a blended family. The nature of the family, however, can become the focus or even the excuse given for any dissatisfaction or miseries.

What needs to be remembered is that a 'good' child may not be a healthy child. Naughtiness and bolshiness at least show energy, creativeness, curiosity and life. And 'bad' behaviour may be more in the eyes of the beholder. You may want to label something the child does or says as bad not because it is wrong but because it unwittingly touches a sore point in you. A new partner may have a misunderstanding with the child and become angry, believing the child has disobeyed deliberately when in fact it may be that he or she has not yet learned or grasped the new adult's rules. What appears to be naughty or rude behaviour may simply be a reasonable response to a dreadfully sad situation. Deirdre recalls being upset by Paul's behaviour at the end of his visits to them.

I thought he was being very ungrateful and rude at first. He was always a very cuddly child and as an adult is just as touchable and touching. But he hates greeting and farewell displays of affection. I think it's because these were just too painful, and reminders for him that he did have a separated family. When he went home, he'd march away and refuse to look back or wave. He's a bit more formally demonstrative – you can kiss him goodbye now – but meeting him at a station you never get the big kissy-style hello. Once home, the chances are he'll snuggle up to either or both of us on a settee.

There is nothing to indicate that there is any difference between the educational attainments of children in blended families and those of children in original families. There may be a temptation for the adults to have lower aspirations for children in a blended family, however, perhaps because stresses and tensions in the home mean that you want them out of your life as soon as possible. Some children may welcome a liberal 'hands off' policy that lets them drop out of school or college or demands little in the way of work achievements. In the long run, however, this is hardly to anyone's advantage.

Children tend to be very accepting of their parents' point of view and less critical of your ideas than you may be of theirs. Most children would like the adults concerned to at least acknowledge that they too often have irrational feelings about what is going on and are not always acting sanely, logically or in the best interests of their children. Paul, now twenty-six, feels that his separated parents had petty quarrels over him that were not fully justified.

I think it is very important for everyone involved to understand that it is not just children who have difficulties in accepting a stepfamily situation, or cause problems by their presence. Quite often I think the continuing relationship of the ex-couple (if there is one) and any new relationship that your parents are coming to terms with (extra-family relationships, if you like) can have a great effect. My own mother and father did, to an extent, get into the 'your son' standard of behaviour over several periods. Not only is this a bloody pain if all you need out of it is a new pair of jeans, but all the unpleasantness and *your* sense of guilt is a result of *their* disagreement as to what makes up their responsibilities. An argument over whose turn it is to buy new clothes is at the bottom end of the scale, but I suppose that in an extreme situation you could end up actually hating one or both parents for what you feel they are making you responsible for.

In the aftermath of the broken relationship children may appear to be startlingly unrealistic. They may harbour the wish, for an unreasonably long time and against all the evidence, that their parents will be reunited at some time in the future. Julie's parents separated seven years ago when she was ten and both have new relationships. For nearly two years after the split Julie hoped it would not be final.

I know I was quite shocked and angry when Dad told me he and Joy were going to have a baby and even more so when my little half-sister was born. All my friends at school thought it was great and couldn't understand the fuss I was making about it. I know what was wrong. It was because up until she came along there was always the chance, and I know this sounds silly, that Mum and Dad would have got together again.

Their hopes for a reunion can sometimes be translated into direct action. Children are perfectly capable of deciding to see off a parent's partner and to wreck the relationship or marriage. This would not be because of malice or cruelty, but because children would genuinely believe they were doing the right thing both for themselves and for their parents. They will think that if any new liaison is removed from the field, what they desire – their parents back together and all the people they love in a happy family again – will come about.

At the same time children can be extraordinarily realistic and even capable of seeing the advantages in a step situation. Twenty-year-old Emma now has a good relationship with her mother's new partner.

> With stepfamilies and single-parent families you've got the perfect opportunity to know your children because you are not sharing them with another person. My stepfather is a great person whom I hold in the highest regard as a friend and mentor, but he's still only a friend. Had my father had a permanent girlfriend from day oneish, then she might have got closer to me – but I would have had four 'parents' then! This would be too much for anyone, especially a small kid. It would be so easy to end up being demanding and getting spoiled in that situation, with everyone trying so hard to protect you. It was great visiting, because my mother and stepfather, who didn't have me around all the time, seemed to have an energy and a capacity for attention that a regular parent can't give.

Paul, who has known Deirdre, his father's partner, for nineteen years, sees her as a 'sort of' third parent and sometimes a distinct advantage. Yet there are pitfalls in reaching that state of affairs.

As for Deirdre, like the relationship with my mother, it's something I wouldn't have missed out on. I don't regard her as my mother or a mother figure (one is enough!) but certainly someone who has some of the 'power' to advise or command attention etc. that a real parent has. However, this is only gained and retained by forming a relationship first. Obviously I couldn't offer any hard and fast rules on how to achieve this other than that both sides involved should consider their own needs and those of the other. In my case, if Deirdre had wanted to become all gooey and become a third parent in the traditional sense, she would have had a nasty shock.

The important thing is to try to create a situation where adaptability is possible. This is something I feel I was part of and provided with, and it's significant that the only time I've felt unhappy is when I felt that my 'step-parent' had been a part of removing this flexible situation. The 'How?' of this is harder to define. It could be by partly using powers that I regard as belonging only to a parent. Certainly what any step-parent should realize is that regardless of what part, if any, they played in the failure of the original relationship, they are part of its aftermath. So if I became cross with my father, then Deirdre *might* be drawn in because she is part of the life he leads that might have caused the problem.

I think it is difficult for some step-parents to appreciate the power of association that they gain in a child's mind by being the partner of one of his or her parents. I would say I love and care for Deirdre, though as a significant friend. It's quite strange for me that I often feel more relaxed with her than with my father, though this is partially due to our characters. In the past this has been upsetting (shouldn't I love/like my father more?), but perhaps this is due to the fact that living with my mother seems to result in my being better at making friends with women. At any rate, it's something that I can deal with and that doesn't bother me. I remind myself that even in a 'normal' family forcing yourself to dispense your attention equally often creates problems and a sense of duty rather than enjoyment and the comfortable situation I was talking about.

It is very easy to forget that adults know from experience that however difficult life may be at present, things may improve. Children have only the past and the present on which to go, and these may both be distressing. You have to put yourself in their shoes in order to understand what they need. Perhaps the most important key to doing this is to listen to what children say rather than steamrollering them and hearing what you would like them to have said. Deirdre regrets not taking some of what Paul said seriously.

Paul used to joke about being a deprived child from a separated home. But I think, in retrospect, the joke was a bit hollow. I think he felt a lot more deprived than he let on, and we were a lot less sensitive than I wish we had been.

6

Making It Work

'The worst thing that happened was one of his daughters not speaking to me for a year. She just couldn't come to terms. In a big family you can skirt round people, and that's what she did. I think she could not admit to herself or anybody else that her father had actually met somebody who was going to be a serious thing in his life. So her way of getting round it was not to talk to the other person involved at all.'

You cannot help what you feel, only what you do about it. As we have already discussed, anyone in a blended family is likely to have a complex range of feelings about themselves, the other people concerned and the situation. Perhaps one of the most important messages we need to absorb is that those feelings, however destructive they are and however much they may distress you, are likely to be natural and normal. If you want to become comfortable with yourself and to reach a working arrangement with everyone else, the first step is to recognize and understand why you feel the way you do. So accept your feelings, even if they are sometimes ones you would rather not own to. You are not to blame for your emotions.

You are, however, in control of the actions you take because of them. Having gained some insight into why a blended family might be so difficult, pinpointed your own fears, angers or anxieties and come to understand how the others might feel, you need to develop strategies for forging an understanding and a working relationship between the adults and the children. Sometimes a 'pre-emptive strike' can nip problems in the bud before they begin. Some people have gone into a blended family so well aware of any difficulties and so well prepared for them that the experience has been no more confusing than being in an average chaotic happy family. But it has to be said that frequently you can recognize a problem only after it is too late. Many eventually happy blended families start off badly or go through difficult periods, so do not despair. There are a number of things you can all do to improve your life together.

This chapter gives practical suggestions as to how you can come to terms with your feelings, discuss them with the rest of your family, get support from friends and other adults and make changes. We will introduce the techniques of discussion, negotiation and compromise and explain how even very young people can take some control over their lives and make their voices heard.

Understanding is not a magic wand. Just because you know why you feel and act the way you do does not mean to say that everything will automatically be better or easier – but it helps. The problem we may have with setting ourselves to the task of understanding is that in our society such exploration is often thought of as raking over painful ashes. This is a bit like believing that you should leave well alone if you cut yourself. If you have a painful wound it is often tempting just to slap a plaster on and do nothing else, because opening up and cleaning the area would hurt so much. Of course, if you did that, the wound might fester and the result might be far more dangerous and painful. Emotional wounds are exactly the same. Only by facing up to what has happened can we heal them and avoid repeating the same mistakes. If you stick your head in the sand like an ostrich and hope nobody can see you, you will probably get run over.

Any blended family by definition arises in the wake of a tragedy and a death – the death of a partner or the death of a relationship. Facing up to and resolving this together is far more likely to bring a better future than trying to block out the past. Second marriages are at a higher risk of ending in divorce, and this may be partly because we rush in with great hopes for the future, refusing to look back at what may still affect us from the past. Children from a disrupted family are at high risk of repeating unhappy patterns later in their own lives, unless their difficulties are recognized and brought out into the open.

In practical terms this means that you will be better off talking than suffering in silence. Whether you are the full-time or part-time birth parent, with or without a new partner, with or without new children through a blended family, you need to establish an open line of communication with every adult and child involved in the new arrangement. If there are problems, they are the responsibility of all the family, even those who seem unaffected by the pressures or difficulties experienced by others. Indeed, if there is a problem of which, on the surface, one member of a family is not aware, the likelihood is that it is this person who needs to share and understand his or her own and everyone else's feelings about what is happening.

Charlie, for instance, holds himself aloof from any of the tensions in his family, saying they have nothing to do with him. His first wife died six years ago, when his son was two and his two daughters were eight and nine. Four years later he married Vicky, who says:

My husband simply doesn't see that we have a problem.

I get on all right with the youngest, but the other two, who are now teenagers, make my life a total hell. On a good day they are just cheeky and take very little notice of me. But most days are bad and they pick quarrels, sulk, swear at me behind my back and are unbelievably vicious and mean. Of course they are all over their daddy and he doesn't see that side of them. Or perhaps it's that he doesn't want to see that side. When I've tried to talk to him about it, he tells me that I've got a problem with the kids and I've to sort it out myself. He doesn't see that the main problem is him and his attitudes. He hates talking about their mother and part of that is because, quite frankly, he hated her, but he won't tell me why. The children, of course, think she was a saint and I'm a total failure in comparison. I haven't a clue what she was really like because it's a taboo subject. A friend of mine said that if I could only get him to talk about her, it might help. But plucking up the courage to do this is my biggest problem.

Everyone in the family has an effect on everyone else and there are no actions that can be taken in isolation. Hit out at one person with whom you are angry or for whom you have no affection and you will also be harming the people you care about and yourself. If only to protect the ones you love, or even out of self-preservation, communication and negotiation are strongly recommended.

Communication is not just a question of getting people to listen to you, it has to be two way. If you want somebody to listen to what you are saying, in return you have to offer to listen to what they are saying. Being able to communicate effectively is not an art we are born with but a skill we develop. For something so important it is appalling that most of us have had very little chance of learning it properly. We are not taught to communicate at school, and often we do not learn communication skills from our parents. So it is something you may have to practise and perfect as an adult.

Many people equate making themselves understood with getting their own way, but proper communication does not lead to just one person's ideas overruling the rest. On the contrary, it leads to negotiation, when everyone has their say and is heard and a final solution is found that satisfies everyone to some extent. A point worthy of note is that after negotiation you may not get precisely what you want, but because everyone gets part of what they want, they are persuaded to go along with the final decision.

In a blended family communication and negotiation are likely to require you to accept possibly difficult conditions. One is that you should include all the adults involved, and that will mean bringing ex-partners and new partners together in some way. The other is that you should take into account the views and needs of the children. If the idea of being in the same county, let alone in the same room, as an ex-partner or their new partner horrifies you, this is obviously going to be distressing. And if you feel that children are too young to give their views, or that you are uncomfortable about listening to them, this too will be hard for you. It may seem false or awkward to sit down together to explain your views or listen to someone else's, but however silly all this sounds, it can be enormously helpful. Ian and Brenda separated two years ago after ten years of marriage. Brenda has been seeing Steven for eighteen months and they have recently bought a house together. Ian and Brenda have two children who live with the new couple. Ian was surprised to receive a phone call from Steven soon after he and Brenda decided to move in together.

Steven rang me up at work and when I realized who he was, I was nearly speechless with rage. He invited me round for a talk and to be honest I went just to tell him what a jumped-up, interfering so-and-so I thought he was. What took the wind out of my sails was that the kids were there round the table too and when I gave him my opinion of him, in a rather strangled speech, he nodded and said yes, he appreciated how I felt. It was quite odd, because I'd expected confrontation and what I got was understanding – very disconcerting. What surprised me was what the kids had to say. I wouldn't have thought an eight- and ten-year-old could have come up with the thoughtful, sensible things they said. I can't exactly say Steven is a best friend, but I have to admit that we do make the best of the situation now.

Deirdre knew James as a friend and first met his son Paul a year before they moved in together. She and James never married, and there was never any other moment to see Paul's mother or make any formal declaration of her relationship with James or his son.

We never actually got together, but James and Laura would ring each other up and from early on if I took the phone call, she'd chat quite happily to me. So it wasn't a round-table discussion ever, but there were discussions. I think I felt awkward at times in that there were things I would have liked to have said that I didn't, but wished I had. But I always had a strong feeling that the line was there. Certainly on the important occasions, when Paul was thought to be seriously ill and when we thought his education was going to have to change tack because of Laura's job in a new town, she was on the phone to James immediately and my opinions were fed back too.

You may need to get clear in your own mind the relative importance of what you want. Some of your demands may be necessities, such as that your children retain contact with both parents and are not forced to divide their loyalties. But other demands are not so much 'needs' as 'wants', such as preferring that they spend Christmas Day with one set of in-laws rather than the other. Once you have put an honest value on your list of requests, you can place them in order of priority and then compare them with everyone else's lists. Negotiation consists in everyone receiving a fair share of what is on offer and all of you gaining and conceding a similar amount.

A set-piece round-the-table discussion between everyone concerned in the new arrangements may be the best way to start off a blended family. It is also a good technique to try if you are having problems and need to clear the air. If you find that such a discussion gets you nowhere or ends in argument, you might consider asking for guidance from a counsellor or conciliator, who is trained to help everyone in a situation to have their say and listen to the others. Addresses are given at the end of the book.

Round-table talks may not always be what you need. There will be plenty of occasions when simply having the time and space to talk to and listen to one other person in the family is what counts, so try to ensure that this is made possible for everyone. Both the new partners and the ex-partners need a chance to share information and share feelings as time goes on.

It may seem strange in a book that is supposed to help you to look after other people's children to say that the first thing you should be doing is looking after yourself. One accusation that is likely to be levelled in broken or blended families is that one or other of you is being selfish. And yet being selfish is another way of being generous – generous to yourself. Indeed, you are not much use to anyone else if you are not cared for as well. So, whether you are the full-time or part-time parent, the new partner in a blended family or on your own or with a new partner, for your own and everyone else's sake you should take some time to pay attention to your own needs.

Keep in touch with friends, and make a point of doing sports or other activities that gave you pleasure in the past. If you have not already got a life outside your immediate family, it would be advisable to build one up. We all need the occasional opportunity to spend time and swap gossip and ideas with our mates, and the possible stresses and strains of a blended family may make this all the more necessary and desirable. Women in a blended family may also find it particularly useful, if possible, to have a part-time or full-time job. Many stepmothers do not work because they are trying to re-create an image of what they see as a 'good, natural family'. In fact, both the adults and the children may benefit from having what is in reality more common and therefore more 'natural', a working mother. A job will give a woman in a blended family what may be much needed outside support. The money may be a considerable help, as will the knowledge that she has a status and a role other than just in the family. Sue is in her late forties and divorced her husband, Jim, when the children were about two. She has looked after the two boys since, though they regularly visit Jim and his partner, Shirley.

Having a job was a godsend in that I didn't really feel shackled to the children. I mean, there was life outside my job as a mum. I think that I ended up liking the children much more because of this. I was very lucky in that I live close to a lot of family and friends, so there were always willing hands for child minding.

Having a career meant a great deal, though it was hard work juggling the two. I had two jobs, I suppose you could say.

The stronger or the more secure the relationship between the new partners, the more that will rebound on the whole new extended family. If you are the parent left behind, it may be tempting to work out your anger and grief at the break-up of your relationship by attacking any weakness you see in the new one. Even if it does not win back the missing partner, at least we may feel satisfied with a measure of revenge. There may be a difficulty, of course, in working out who is the loser, since it is often the children who suffer most in such a battle. You may therefore consider that the stability of the new relationship may be just as much in your interests as the couple's, and is certainly in your children's interests. It may seem odd for someone to be making a case for the ex-partner to support a new relationship, but for your own and your children's continuing happiness this may be your best option, as Sue has discovered.

I don't think that Shirley and I see each other as a threat, and when we all get together for birthdays and such we get on very well, especially when Jim's not around. I'm glad that we are relatively happy and still talking, all taking pleasure from looking after and enjoying the company of our children. If you are going to do something 'for the sake of the children', then you've got to do what you say.

If you are in the new relationship yourself, you are probably determined that it succeeds. You may like to consider the suggestion that while relationships break up for many and varied reasons, rarely can it be said to be one person's fault. What is important is sharing responsibility for the breakdown of communication. If you do not want this to happen again, it may be best to resolve that you and your partner make a determined effort to understand yourselves and each other, and to talk to each other as much as possible. If you have any difficulties, seek help to resolve them at an early stage, rather than leaving it until it is again too late.

Children need both their parents, whatever the circumstances of the split between these two adults. To retain the sense of their own identity and to maintain the secure feeling that all is right with the world, they need to know their mother and father are there for them, even though they cannot see both of them every day. If you have had a child, even if you did not choose to become a parent at that point in your life and with that particular person, you too need to keep the link with the child who bears your genes for your own comfort and well-being. So it is vital that everyone seeks all possible means to sustain the relationship between both parents and their children, however difficult and painful this may seem. Any distress is more likely to be the result of making that contact difficult than integral to the relationship and the situation. If you make it easier to maintain contact, it will be more comfortable.

When parents have split up, however, more emphasis is generally laid on the relationship between each parent and any children. This may be partly because each one spends more time with the child than he or she might otherwise have done, or that the time together consists of quite concentrated one-to-one experiences. Parents may then lean and rely too heavily on the children, and treat them like substitute adults. Never forget that, whatever your problems, you are an adult and the children are children. Sharing inappropriate confidences with them, especially about your sex life, puts unfair pressures on the children. Saying 'We are just like sisters/friends' might sound wonderful, but a parent should always be a parent and recognize boundaries. Drawing the children on to adult territory may make it difficult for them to detach themselves from you as they get older and is likely to cause resentment and jealousy if a new partner comes along. But it is often extremely helpful for children to have at least some idea of your feelings and attitudes. Never showing grief, anger or resentment can give them the wrong idea about your emotions and the impression that you simply do not care. The answer is to strike a balance, and to walk the fine line between keeping them in the dark and shining too bright a light on them.

Perhaps one advantage of a split family is that it requires parents to make time to spend with their children. On Sundays parks and museums tend to be full of separated parents and their children having their one-day visit together. While special treats may be welcomed by children, however, everyday experiences together are more important. Most children would be glad of the opportunity to simply be with their parent – sitting around at home even if it is an untidy bedsit, and sharing in ordinary chores such as shopping and cooking.

However painful it may be to recall experiences in the first relationship, adults and children will find it extremely valuable. All children want to know where they came from and if you shy away from talking about the past, either to protect your own, your new partner's or your children's feelings, you will be doing everyone a disservice. Cutting out the past could give a painful message to a child – that half his or her very self is unacceptable. So do not be afraid of looking at photos or saying 'Do you remember when . . .?' If anyone in your blended family has anxieties about this, it is better to get them out in the open and talk them over

than to bury them. For the well-being of the entire new extended family it is essential to help children keep their good
feelings about both parents. Explain that adults can have
differences that have nothing to do with the children and
recognize the importance of the other parent, whatever your
own opinion.

If a blended family is to succeed and children are to
accept and be accepted by the new adults involved, perhaps
the first and most fundamental step is not to try to conform
to any idealized myth of 'the family'. You cannot expect
everything to be straightforward, and there will be conflict
and pain, as there is in any family.

Some step-parents, in an effort to endear themselves to
the children, slip into the habit of being too nice, making
every effort to give them their favourite foods and not
expecting them to do chores. This is particularly prevalent
in stepfamilies where children visit for a limited time. The
problem is that this behaviour emphasizes that the children
are visitors and that the situation is unusual. Children and
adults need to feel that they have an everyday relationship,
and the only way to do that is for everyone to behave as
normal. This includes being able to make demands and
occasionally become angry. Otherwise resentments will build
up and expand out of all proportion. By all means spare the
rod, but do not shy away from natural confrontations with
a stepchild.

Rather than trying to pretend you are 'a normal family',
try to make a virtue of your extra family, the diversity and
spread of contacts. In many communities, both in the past
and in the present, people live in far larger groups, which
has its advantages. After all, when two parents are living
together with their children, there may be times when they
have their own concerns and cannot spare time for each
other. When you have what Carol and Philip, with his four

children from a previous marriage and two of their own, call 'an amorphous, extended family', you can find there is always somebody free to listen or talk to you.

A new step-parent can help, in being much better than the alternative of a lone parent. Marvin's parents split up ten years ago when he was eleven. His mother was on her own for two years before she started living with her boyfriend.

She got quite ill after my dad left, with various illnesses related to depression. It was very tough to see her having to put up with the fact that my dad had moved in with someone else. And that he'd got someone there for him if he had problems. I was glad when Keith came along. It brought my mum out of a very bad period. There wasn't anything I could do, really. You can say, 'Mum, I think you're great', but it doesn't help at the time. The fact that Keith didn't try to say, 'Look, forget your other dad, I'm the new man about the house', and acted as my mum's boyfriend allowed us to get along.

Whether the parent's new partner becomes a full-time or a part-time person in the child's life, he or she will have a considerable impact. This can be enormously beneficial if handled sensitively. Perhaps the most helpful advice given by people who have made it work is to try not to replace a parent but to become an additional adult on the scene – a significant friend. Matthew lives with his father and his second wife, Marian. He and Marian enjoy each other's company.

It's good to have someone there you can trust quite well and talk to. You can be honest with them because they're not your parents and at the end of the day don't care what you do. They have no sort of real attachment to you. I think of her as an adult, but as a friend as well. We've never had any real problems, because I'd known her for ages. It was good to get to know her before any commitment was made. There's no pressure on you at all to have to like this person first, so you can take them as they are. I owe quite a lot to Marian for its being an excellent situation at Dad's. If there was a wedding or at my graduation or some other family occasion, I don't think Mum would have a problem with Marian coming. She can cope for one day, and if she didn't I'd be very offended. Marian doesn't try to be my mother at all, and I think that's why it works between us. We have a sort of understanding. It's her house, and I'm living with her because she's married to Dad, but she doesn't try to control me in any particular way. She doesn't try to impress her ideas on my life and she doesn't say 'You must do this, you must do that' like a parent would. She's helpful, more like a friend. She does have an element of power because it's her house, but it's Dad who says where the buck stops. If she did try to do that, I'd say it was fairly reasonable if, for instance, I can't be bothered to do the washing-up, stuff like that, and she got pissed off at me. She says, 'Bloody hell, Matthew, get a grip.'

Marvin's mother has been living with her new partner for eight years, and he and Marvin get on well together.

I don't treat him as a stepdad. It works brilliantly and we go out and down to the pub together. If my dad had died, maybe it would have been different, but I've got a dad there and even if I don't see him, he's my father.

Patently a new partner will have taken the place of one

parent in the other parent's life, but if he or she clearly does not intend to replace the parent in the child's life, and indeed on occasion is actively helpful, the 'abandoned' parent may be able to see the situation in constructive terms. Sue, like some other lone parents, has found her ex's new partner is able to have a role in her children's lives that is a positive asset.

Shirley never told me how to look after my children, other than being part of the parental grapevine that helped me know how the boys were doing. In a way, I'm glad she was around for them. She's younger than Jim and so more like a friend than an adult, which is something that the boys seem to appreciate. If anybody has to watch out, it's Jim, because I often hear the boys say they get on better with her even though they love their father very much. Obviously I'd like to be still married to the father of my sons, but that didn't work out, so we made the best of the situation.

It is significant that stepmothers are often much younger than their husband's first partner. This can be an advantage for any children involved, and much easier for the new adult, in that it makes it possible to put the relationship on to an equal footing and she can take the role of a 'sister' who is fun to be with. Deirdre found herself capitalizing on the fact that she is twelve years younger than her partner, James, and so only sixteen years older than his son, as she got to know him.

I knew James first as a friend and then as a flatmate, and I met Paul when he was seven. He would come to stay for weekends, and sometimes for longer. I think we always got on when he was little. I never talk down to young people and I do play – you know, get down on the floor and muck about, and run around in parks without worrying about my hair or make-up. We have some super photos of Paul and me laughing like idiots, throwing snowballs, eating ice-cream and generally acting like clowns. I don't think I did it deliberately, but I took the role of a big sister rather than trying to be a mother to him, and that meant he didn't have much reason to resent me or to feel a clash of loyalties.

Jack has found the same advantage: he is seventeen and his father's new wife in her thirties.

My stepmum's upbringing was a lot more like my own. I could almost see her as a sister. It's strange, she's really fun to be with. She's not ashamed to be rude or childish, and, unlike my stepfather, she likes a lot of the things I do. I also think she has managed to cope with having 'new kids' much better than my stepfather has. It's quite fun to have two families, as it were. I think stepfamilies do get a sort of advantage, especially the kids. Instead of a 'perfect' family and 'perfect' parents, you get to see the nastier side of life when you are younger and maybe get better prepared for it later on.

If, as the step-parent, you are not prepared to make the effort to make it work, then perhaps you should be having second thoughts about this relationship. If you cannot accept the idea of the children, maybe you should turn back. The children cannot walk away and, after all, they were there first. But if you decide to join, try not to set yourself unreasonably high targets. Do not expect to love the children at once and do not feel guilty if love never grows on your side or theirs. Parents are not always good, right, loving and caring. They too may find it takes some time to get to know and like, let alone love, their offspring. Remember, however, that some children come to a step-parent with a sigh of relief and in that relationship find a special type of parental love for the first time in their lives; they leave (or never really leave) with deep gratitude. Author David Gemmell put the following dedication in one of his books:

> Some men climb mountains, or found empires, others make fortunes or create classics. But *Quest for Lost Heroes* is dedicated with love to Bill Woodford, who took on the role of stepfather to a shy, introverted and illegitimate six-year-old boy, and never once let him down. Through his patient encouragement, his quiet strength and his endless affection he gave his son the pride and the confidence to fight his own battles – both in life and on the printed page. Thanks, Dad!

Obviously when two people come together and both already have children to bring to the relationship, the situation can be like a Chinese puzzle – links in a tangled chain. Both parents will be in the situation of being a step-parent and a parent coping with their former partner, their own children and the new step-parent. The children themselves will have to deal not only with the separation of their parents and coming to terms with the new adult but also with step-siblings. This can be confusing. Moira was extremely excited at the prospect of she and her brother having a new older brother when her mother, Jane, married Adrian.

> We met Ian quite a few times before Adrian and Mum got married. He's nice and I like him. But since the marriage he has changed completely. We've only seen him twice and he completely ignored Roy and me. Now he won't visit at all and I think that's sad. It's

funny, because we've lost two brothers; our older brother, Steven, who lives with our father, also refuses to talk to us now ever since the marriage.

Children born to the new partnership introduce a new balance, which may be either helpful or destructive. Carol and Philip found his children welcomed the births of their own two children.

It's actually made for a better situation at home. It seems to make people happier. They all came up from wherever they were within a few days of the births. We were thrilled about that. I would almost have understood if they had stayed away. It's one thing for Father to have a younger girlfriend and live with her, but it's quite another for them to start having kids all over again at his age. They were so delighted, and very loving and attentive with the two kids involved, so that's been very, very good. I love the children who came to me with my husband and like them very much. But having two children who were my own was very important.

Marvin, whose stepmother is expecting her first baby, is planning to visit for the birth.

I'm actually quite looking forward to it. I know I won't see him/her very often, but a new half-brother or half-sister is something I didn't expect would happen. I think she's getting a bit old for it, but I would really like it if my mum had another child. It wouldn't bother me at all, but I can't see it happening. They haven't got a piece of paper saying they are married, so a child would be a sort of symbol.

Turning now to the question of the other parent, it is

worth noting that around half of remarried men keep in touch with their first wives. Just as children are yours for life, so the other parent remains. Children have a right to retain links with both original parents and unless you can swallow your anger, pride or envy, you and they will suffer. To think that getting rid of the old partner, leaving the field clear, will improve the new relationship is misguided. On the contrary, there will be a better relationship within the blended family and between the new partners when relations with the other parent are good too. Children in all families have relationships with adults outside the family circle – we can call these chosen adults. Needing such friendships does not cast doubt on the parents' ability or put their authority or parenting skills in question. So, still respecting, loving and needing the other original parent does not put at risk the relationship the new partners have with each other, or the stepchild might develop with the new partner.

It is important not to become competitive with the other partner or their new partner. Adults may want to use treats to buy love, or at least the appearance of love, and needy, anxious children are prone to grabbing these displays and boasting about them to others. What the child is saying is, 'They love me, because they buy me things. Do you love me too?' You can say yes without having to get out your wallet to prove it and, in time, the child will grow up enough to recognize what is going on.

Rather than expecting anyone – your friends, your relatives, the children themselves – to take sides, try to make them see all of you and your situation as common, natural and neutral. It may be helpful to ask the wider family to make an effort to do this and not to put undue extra pressure on an already delicate situation. If they will not or cannot put aside their personal feelings, the best tack is to make this clear to the children so that they can understand that everyone holds different opinions.

You may find it necessary to ask the family to treat all children in your blended family the same and explain that you will not stand for divisiveness. Of course, you must take the same approach yourself and not treat your 'own' children differently from any new children of the blended family.

What is the very worst picture of your re-formed family you can imagine? Continued arguments, perpetual disagreements, sustained hostility? Whatever your situation at the moment, by doing nothing you are probably encouraging your fears to materialize. By taking action, however painful, you could have the opportunity to direct matters. Taking the initiative is at the core of any successful relationship, and it is advisable not to listen to the myths that say tinkering with it only makes it worse. There are quite a few practical actions you could take that might contribute to a stress-free blended family.

One is recognizing the importance of making a will. This may not only forestall the painful results of an unexpected death but also help in establishing a framework for the relationship of a child and new adult. Deirdre made her stepson, Paul, her next of kin and feels this move was part of a new, stronger relationship between them.

> Paul is the least materialistic person I know, but when we moved to our new house, when he was about twenty-one, I made a point of having a fresh will drawn up. This makes him the designated next of kin to both myself and James after each other. The money is nothing to him, but when I told him what I'd done, I'm sure he was pleased. I was saying, in no uncertain terms, that he is the next most special person to me after his father, and I mean it.

Parents may have to agree on their attitudes to details

such as consent to medical treatment, foreign travel, obtaining a passport, education and religious affiliation. The non-residential parent still has a say in a child's life, but this must be used to keep concerned involvement, not to complicate matters or compromise the child's well-being. Strictly speaking, a parent's new partner is not *in loco parentis* even if he or she is caring for the child full time and would therefore be unable to give consent for medical treatment, for example, which could be inconvenient in some circumstances and dangerous in others.

You may need to discuss the arrangements for legal responsibility and residence of the children. Consider whether it is sufficient to settle on an arrangement – a so-called gentlemen's agreement – or whether it is necessary to go to court for a residence order or even to apply for adoption. You may feel that adoption would be the best way of achieving stability, but the courts are highly unlikely to allow it unless there is no other way of acting in the child's best interests. A counsellor or conciliator may help you, both to understand and accept the legalities and to hear the views of everyone concerned.

All the adults involved also need to decide what they want to happen in the event of a tragedy. If one parent dies, is it assumed that the child will automatically live with the other? If the children have lived with one parent and a new partner, will they stay in that home in the event of that parent dying? The views of even very young children should be taken into account when you are debating these difficult and painful decisions, and you would be advised to ask for the guidance of a counsellor or a conciliator. It is a very human failing to avoid talking about tragedy in the superstitious belief that if you do not mention it, it will not happen, and if you do talk about it, it will. If you leave such important decisions to fate and they then have to be settled by law, you might find that the rigid, official rulings may not be in everyone's best interests. Remember that, in law, the step-parent in the partnership has no rights over the children whatsoever unless these have been negotiated and officially agreed. Many pitfalls can be avoided if you make the proper provisions for them, and it would be worth rereading the discussion of legal matters in Chapter 2. Make sure that you have not left your family or yourself vulnerable should the worst happen, and if necessary seek professional advice.

You may benefit from using counselling or conciliation to help you cope with the demands of the new extended family, whatever role you play in it. Christine, who married Gregory and found herself with three stepchildren who stayed once a fortnight, has found her counselling and support network invaluable.

> I happen to be, and have been for ten years now, in a women's therapy group where by coincidence all five of us are stepmothers. In fact, all of us are also mostly part-time stepmothers. I've had tremendous support from these other women. We also have friends whom we talk to a lot, but that is informal. If we didn't have that, I'd want some formal support.

As already discussed, living arrangements make an enormous difference to the success of a new extended family. Studies have shown that when parents have split up and children are dividing time between them, their chances of achieving happiness and stability are dramatically increased if the two households are within walking or cycling distance. A child can then choose when and if to see the other parent and can call in at times other than those formally arranged. If this is not possible, it is essential that they at least feel they have a place in both households. If there is not enough space for part-time children to have their own room, try to find a corner that they can think of as theirs, where belongings can be safely left until their next visit.

How you divide up the living space itself can be important. If you cannot move house, so that everyone starts again on an equal footing, one tip is to move round all the bedrooms in the house so that everyone starts with a new room. The defence of territory is such a basic instinct, even with the very young, that you have to make allowances for and understand these feelings. If you have not already laid down the rule that in your household children have a right to privacy in their own space and that even adults should ask permission and knock before entering, you may find it helpful to introduce this now.

Children have no say in the dissolution of their original family and the establishment of the new one. They are not offered any compromises – the old family is splitting up and the new one is being established whether they like it or not. But straightaway they have to compromise by sharing a room or accepting the presence in their living space of people they have not chosen. Their feelings of powerlessness can be overwhelming and may lead to depressive or destructive behaviour. Try to give them some sort of control over their lives – even if it is only the right to choose the family's supper menu one night a week.

It helps, of course, if you are prepared to talk over and explain your decisions and to ask for and accept some measure of feedback from the children. The balance is a delicate one, though. Children's priorities are different from those of adults, and if you look at it simply in terms of 'asking permission' from your children, you may find yourself in a very unhappy situation. You need to tread the fine line between patronizing children and instituting your decisions under the guise of 'what is best for them', and indulging them and allowing an emotional desire of the moment to supersede their long-term interests. By all means use your experience in judging when to apply your authority, but listen to and acknowledge their ideas as well.

If a process of explanation and discussion is to take place with the children, make sure all of them are involved. If you cannot adjust your thinking to see all of them as equal, at least accept that without guilt. John has great difficulties with Nigel, his wife's son by her first marriage, who lives with his father but visits regularly. The relationship was tolerable until John and Anna had children of their own, but it has since deteriorated.

> I find him annoying and after a couple of days of staying with us he really gets on my nerves. I'm sure Nigel feels rather confused and unloved by the situation, but that simply isn't my problem. My own three children are the ones I really put first. I used to feel very guilty and inadequate about the way I felt about Nigel. For a long time I pretended there wasn't a problem, but of course that made it worse. Now that at least I'm recognizing my feelings and I'm discussing them with Anna, the heat seems to have gone out of the situation.

You will need to agree rules, values and standards with the children and the other adults concerned. Discuss your views on discipline and behaviour within and outside the home. It is obviously easier if these are both similar and consistent and you can come to an agreement. You may well find that you have differences, however, which is not necessarily a problem as long as you agree to differ and explain why, trying not to undermine each other. If you must dwell on the differences between parents and households, at least make this not a judgement but a reflection. You can present children, and indeed other adults, with the valuable lesson that people can disagree on the principles even though they have the same priority, a concern for the children's well-being. Whether you are in agreement or not, it is helpful for children living with you full or part time if you make the ground rules clear.

Of course, occasionally you may need to accept that too much worrying and analysing is counter-productive. Carol says she sometimes feels the best thing she could have had, to deal with her partner Philip's four children, was

> a one-way ticket on a banana boat! It would have been easier to handle the situation if we had never bothered. If I'd known some of the difficulties, some of the things that make you cry and some of the things that make you want to run off down the road. But I'm not a negative person. If I'd known some of them or two thirds of them, I might have thought this is not for me.

One particular area of uncertainty among children is who exactly has the right to lay down the law to them. The assumption in our society is that only a parent or someone 'licensed' by them, such as a teacher, can do so. If children have mixed feelings about the role of a parent's partner in their lives, they will wish to contest the right of this adult to tell them what to do. One convenient distinction to make is that partners may not be parents but in their home children must obey their rules. You may also introduce the concept of simple, natural courtesy: bad, boorish behaviour is something that anyone has the right to object to, parent or not.

After a period of disruption children may find it difficult to return to having routines and fixed schedules, and they may object if you try to establish these. On the other hand, you may find children – especially visiting, part-time children – insist on a set programme or pattern. Long after you would like a bit of variety, they may be clinging to the familiar and known. Children may ask for the same bedtime story, the same evening meal, the same, unvarying, day out. Routines give children an enormous measure of security, so discuss them with everyone and ensure they are established and maintained.

It may be impossible to ensure that everyone in your family gets what they want and need. Perhaps if you can begin with the conviction that the emotional growth and stability of every member of your family is as important as everyone else's, you may get close to achieving the best compromise. Try to avoid having either martyrs or scape-goats. It does not help for you to sacrifice your own needs and interests in order to make someone else happy, nor should you pick on one person and act as if all the problems are entirely his or her fault.

If children only visit you or stay occasionally, it can be easy to fall into the treat trap. Because their visit is a limited and eagerly anticipated occasion, you may want to mark it with a relaxation of the usual demands and to celebrate. Unfortunately, this only serves to underline the out-of-the-ordinary nature of your relationship. It puts unfair pressure on the child, and on the other parent. Deirdre and James saw his son at weekends or during his school holidays, when they would take leave from work. Deirdre would make a point of filling up the fridge with his favourite drinks, cooking the foods he requested and taking him out to special events.

Paul said to me a couple of times that he wished he lived with us full time, and I know Laura used to get quite exasperated at the little brat going home and going on for hours about the wonderful time he'd had. I had the sense, one time, to point out to him that if he did live with us, it would be very different and just like living at home. After that visit, I tried to act a little less special, like telling him to get his own drink from the fridge when he wanted one rather than getting it for him.

Part-time children should help around their part-time home, and have chores, if it is to be like a home and not a hotel. For the same reasons, feed them what you would eat yourselves – no special adult treats and no junk diets either. Food has a symbolic place in our society. We offer food as a proof of love, and eat it sometimes to comfort or reward ourselves. We often also reject food as a way of punishing ourselves or the person giving it. It has a powerful role in all families and particularly families with any sort of problem.

All sorts of things we say or do have a deeper and wider meaning. Our actions are often symbolic – that is, they stand in for an unstated and often unrecognized communication. The problem is that we frequently misunderstand each other's hidden message. We can find ourselves carrying on a whole 'conversation' without saying a word, and in two or more different languages. Mark's mother remarried when he was thirteen, and her new husband had two daughters of his own.

My stepfather and I didn't get on for years. He'd fixed up a room for me when we went to live with them, and it seemed to me to be like a boxroom, full of all sorts of rubbish – an old cricket bat and trashy old comics and pictures. His daughters had brand-new stuff. I was resentful and he seemed to take against me at once. It took us ages to get on good terms. Years later he told me that all that gear was treasured stuff he'd saved from his own childhood and he'd wanted for ages to have a son to give it to. I was that son – except I'd rejected his presents and he felt so hurt and angry.

Poor old Dad! It just goes to show that you don't think of grown-ups as having feelings, do you?

It may sound silly to have to explain yourself and to ask children what they mean by doing something, but it could prevent a surprising number of difficulties.

The step-relationship has some advantages over the natural child–parent relationship. You can make a virtue of the fact that step-children and parents sometimes know each other better than birth parents and children – you can approach another person's child as a real person rather than as an extension of yourself. You may find it difficult to love them, but you can respect and ultimately care for them. Rather than trying to cover up the differences between original and blended families, you can celebrate them. For instance, allow children to make their own choice of surname and to pick the name they will call their parent's partner, and do not see it as a triumph or a failure, whichever role you play and whichever name they choose.

Above all, you must never expect gratitude. Appreciation, recognition and respect may come, as may love. And gratitude may be offered in time. But all have to be earned and it is a two-way process. You should be prepared to give everything you would like in return.

After the warnings, suggestions and reflections, the final word is that it can work. When asked to describe the best thing about being in a blended family, Paul, Christine and Deirdre replied as follows:

The best thing was having three loving 'parents' – being spoiled and enjoying every minute (well, most of it). Since it works in most ways, who could ask for more?

The best times? Oh, the sheer enjoyment of suddenly having this family – the trips out and juice in bed in the morning. Lovely, warm family things just the same as any other family.

One lovely incident was when we went to collect Paul for a weekend with us. We saw him from the far end of the street, playing on the pavement. As we got nearer, he saw us and came running. You can picture the scene, like one of those movies where a couple start at each end of the beach and run in slow motion towards each other. He hurtled up, James bent down with his arms open and Paul flung himself . . . into my arms.

Appendix:

Useful Addresses

Most of the following addresses and telephone numbers are of the organizations' main offices. Check your local phone book first, and if there is no entry, contact the head office for the address of the nearest local help that is available.

British Association for
  Counselling
1 Regent Place
Rugby
Warwickshire CV21 2PJ
(0788 578328/9)

Catholic Marriage Advisory
  Council
Clitherow House
1 Blythe Mews
Blythe Road
London W14 0NW
(071 371 1341)

Child Guidance Clinics – see
  under Child and Family
  Guidance in your local phone
  book

Citizens Advice Bureau – see
  your local phone book

Divorce Conciliation and
  Advisory Service
38 Ebury Street
London SW1 0LU
(071 730 2422)

Gingerbread
35 Wellington Street
London WC2E 7BN
(071 240 0953)

Institute of Family Therapy
43 New Cavendish Street
London W1M 7RG
(071 935 2946)

National Council for One
  Parent Families
255 Kentish Town Road
London NW5 2LX
(071 237 1361)

National Family Conciliation
  Council
34 Milton Road
Swindon SN1 5JA
(0793 514055)

National Stepfamily
  Association
72 Willesden Lane
London NW6 7TA
(071 372 0844)

Northern Ireland Marriage
  Guidance Council
76 Dublin Road
Belfast BT2 7HP
(0232 323454)

Parent Network
44–46 Caversham Road
London NW5 2DS
(071 485 8535)

Relate
Herbert Gray College
Little Church Street
Rugby CV21 3AP
(0788 73241)

Scottish Marriage Guidance
  Council
26 Frederick Street
Edinburgh EH2 2JR
(031 255 5006)

Solicitors' Family Law
  Association
154 Fleet Street
London EC4A 2HX

Discover more about our forthcoming books through Penguin's FREE newspaper...

Penguin
Quarterly

It's packed with:

- exciting features
- author interviews
- previews & reviews
- books from your favourite films & TV series
- exclusive competitions & much, much more...

READ MORE IN PENGUIN

In every corner of the world, on every subject under the sun, Penguin represents quality and variety – the very best in publishing today.

For complete information about books available from Penguin – including Puffins, Penguin Classics and Arkana – and how to order them, write to us at the appropriate address below. Please note that for copyright reasons the selection of books varies from country to country.

In the United Kingdom: Please write to *Dept. JC, Penguin Books Ltd, FREEPOST, West Drayton, Middlesex UB7 OBR*

If you have any difficulty in obtaining a title, please send your order with the correct money, plus ten per cent for postage and packaging, to *PO Box No. 11, West Drayton, Middlesex UB7 OBR*

In the United States: Please write to *Penguin USA Inc., 375 Hudson Street, New York, NY 10014*

In Canada: Please write to *Penguin Books Canada Ltd, 10 Alcorn Avenue, Suite 300, Toronto, Ontario M4V 3B2*

In Australia: Please write to *Penguin Books Australia Ltd, 487 Maroondah Highway, Ringwood, Victoria 3134*

In New Zealand: Please write to *Penguin Books (NZ) Ltd,182–190 Wairau Road, Private Bag, Takapuna, Auckland 9*

In India: Please write to *Penguin Books India Pvt Ltd, 706 Eros Apartments, 56 Nehru Place, New Delhi 110 019*

In the Netherlands: Please write to *Penguin Books Netherlands B.V., Keizersgracht 231 NL–1016 DV Amsterdam*

In Germany: Please write to *Penguin Books Deutschland GmbH, Friedrichstrasse 10–12, W–6000 Frankfurt/Main 1*

In Spain: Please write to *Penguin Books S. A., C. San Bernardo 117–6° E–28015 Madrid*

In Italy: Please write to *Penguin Italia s.r.l., Via Felice Casati 20, 1–20124 Milano*

In France: Please write to *Penguin France S. A., 17 rue Lejeune, F–31000 Toulouse*

In Japan: Please write to *Penguin Books Japan, Ishikiribashi Building, 2–5–4, Suido, Bunkyo-ku, Tokyo 112*

In Greece: Please write to *Penguin Hellas Ltd, Dimocritou 3, GR–106 71 Athens*

In South Africa: Please write to *Longman Penguin Southern Africa (Pty) Ltd, Private Bag X08, Bertsham 2013*

READ MORE IN PENGUIN

A SELECTION OF HEALTH BOOKS

The Kind Food Guide Audrey Eyton

Audrey Eyton's all-time bestselling *The F-Plan Diet* turned the nation on to fibre-rich food. Now, as the tide turns against factory farming, she provides the guide destined to bring in a new era of eating.

Baby and Child Penelope Leach

A beautifully illustrated and comprehensive handbook on the first five years of life. 'It stands head and shoulders above anything else available at the moment' – Mary Kenny in the *Spectator*

Woman's Experience of Sex Sheila Kitzinger

Fully illustrated with photographs and line drawings, this book explores the riches of women's sexuality at every stage of life. 'A book which any mother could confidently pass on to her daughter – and her partner too' – *Sunday Times*

A Guide to Common Illnesses Dr Ruth Lever

The complete, up-to-date guide to common complaints and their treatment, from causes and symptoms to cures, explaining both orthodox and complementary approaches.

Living with Alzheimer's Disease and Similar Conditions
Dr Gordon Wilcock

This complete and compassionate self-help guide is designed for families and carers (professional or otherwise) faced with the 'living bereavement' of dementia.

Living with Stress
Cary L. Cooper, Rachel D. Cooper and Lynn H. Eaker

Stress leads to more stress, and the authors of this helpful book show why low levels of stress are desirable and how best we can achieve them in today's world. Looking at those most vulnerable, they demonstrate ways of breaking the vicious circle that can ruin lives.

READ MORE IN PENGUIN

A SELECTION OF HEALTH BOOKS

Living with Asthma and Hay Fever John Donaldson

For the first time, there are now medicines that can prevent asthma attacks from taking place. Based on up-to-date research, this book shows how the majority of sufferers can beat asthma and hay fever to lead full and active lives.

Anorexia Nervosa R. L. Palmer

Lucid and sympathetic guidance for those who suffer from this disturbing illness and their families and professional helpers, given with a clarity and compassion that will make anorexia more understandable and consequently less frightening for everyone involved.

Medical Treatments: Benefits and Risks Peter Parish

The ultimate reference guide to the drug treatments available today – from over-the-counter remedies to drugs given under close medical supervision – for every common disease or complaint from acne to worms.

Pregnancy and Childbirth Sheila Kitzinger
Revised Edition

A complete and up-to-date guide to physical and emotional preparation for pregnancy – a must for all prospective parents.

Miscarriage Ann Oakley, Ann McPherson and Helen Roberts

One million women worldwide become pregnant every day. At least half of these pregnancies end in miscarriage or stillbirth. But each miscarriage is the loss of a potential baby, and that loss can be painful to adjust to. Here is sympathetic support and up-to-date information on one of the commonest areas of women's reproductive experience.

The Parents' A-Z Penelope Leach

For anyone with children of 6 months, 6 years or 16 years, this guide to all the little problems in their health, growth and happiness will prove reassuring and helpful.

BY THE SAME AUTHOR

Endometriosis

'Anyone who has endometriosis – or who suspects they might have – will be glad of Suzie Hayman's clear explanation of the condition and its treatment. Endometriosis is a baffling and complicated illness; this book offers both information and hope' – Hilary Mantel

In this positive and practical book Suzie Hayman tells you:

● What endometriosis is
● Why it occurs
● How it affects you
● How it can be diagnosed, treated and managed
● Self-help methods and complementary treatment
● How drugs and surgery can help

Her book provides both sufferers and their doctors with the information necessary for an improved understanding of this frequently puzzling condition.

The Well Woman Handbook

A guide for women throughout their lives

Bodies like machines need regular attention to keep them in a healthy state. Yet many of us see health care in terms of cure rather than prevention and are content to leave it to the medical professionals.

The concept of Well Woman care challenges this view and shows how women can take control of their own bodies.

This holistic approach to health care means looking at your whole lifestyle – diet, work, leisure, relationships and environment – and considering how these affect your total wellbeing. Practical and informative, *The Well Woman Handbook* will enable you to learn more about your body and put the responsibility for its health back into your own hands.

● Getting to know your body
● What can go wrong
● Practical steps to put it right
● Consulting professionals
● Considering your lifestyle